THIS IS HOW YOU MAKE A MOVIE

KU-538-741

LAURENCE KING

Published in 2021 by
Laurence King Publishing Ltd
361–373 City Road
London EC1V 1LR
United Kingdom
enquiries@laurenceking.com
www.laurenceking.com

© Text 2021 Tim Grierson

Tim Grierson has asserted his right under
the Copyright, Designs and Patents Act 1988
to be identified as the Author of this Work.

All rights reserved. No part of this publication
may be reproduced or transmitted in any form
or by any means, electronic or mechanical,
including photocopying, recording or any
information storage or retrieval system, without
prior permission in writing from the publisher.

A catalogue record for this book is available
from the British Library

ISBN: 978 1 78627 558 5

Design: Florian Michelet
Commissioning Editor: Zara Larcombe
Senior Editor: Felicity Maunder

Printed in China

Laurence King Publishing is committed to
ethical and sustainable production. We are
proud participants in The Book Chain Project®
bookchainproject.com

BOOK CHAIN PROJECT

10081141
Luton Sixth Form College
Learning Resources Centre
791.430232

Image captions, openers:

ACTING (pages 8–9): Al Pacino and Brian
De Palma on the set of *Scarface*, 1983

DIRECTING (pages 34–5): Alfred
Hitchcock with Grace Kelly on the set
of *Rear Window*, 1953

LIGHTING & CAMERA (pages 84–5):
William Daniels and Jacques Feyder with
Greta Garbo on the set of *The Kiss*, 1929

EDITING (pages 138–9): Director Steven
Spielberg and editor Michael Kahn in
the editing suite during the making of
Poltergeist, 1981

WRITING (pages 160–61): Neil Simon
at the typewriter, 1967

791.430232

Luton Sixth Form College
Learning Resources Centre

Luton Sixth Form College

Bradgers Hill Road

Luton LU2 7EW

Telephone 01582 432480 email: library@lutonsfc.ac.uk

Return on or before the last date stamped below

2 1 FEB 2022

0 5 JAN 2022

10081141

Luton Sixth Form College

THIS IS HOW YOU MAKE A MOVIE

Tim Grierson

Laurence King Publishing

Contents

Introduction

In an era in which the internet, social media, portable digital cameras and affordable editing software have allowed many more people to try their hand at filmmaking than ever before, the creative possibilities are endless for those hungry to tell their stories. But what hasn't changed is the need to understand the basics of the craft – to learn the building blocks of cinema in order to incorporate them into your art.

A book titled *This Is How You Make a Movie* is risking immodesty, but what I hope this collection of tutorials ends up demonstrating is that, in fact, there is no one way to make a movie. Over more than a century, directors have been expanding the terrain of what constitutes a great film, relying on foundational techniques while, at the same time, developing bold new ways of thinking about a medium that is in constant flux. What I've set out to do with this book is provide an overview of some of cinema's core elements – screenwriting, acting, shooting, postproduction – by selecting classic and contemporary films that highlight important principles. But as you'll see, grasping the fundamentals is merely the beginning: Some of my examples proudly break or subvert the rules. Budding filmmakers should be encouraged to do the same.

Along the way, perhaps you'll be interested in expanding your own cultural palate. I've included everything from blockbusters (*Wonder Woman*) to Oscar-winners (*Rocky*), silent-era gems (*Intolerance*) to recent art-house treasures (*American Honey*), to give readers a glimpse of cinema's breadth and potential. Films from Sweden, Mexico, the UK, Iran, France, the USA, Italy and elsewhere are represented, with an eye toward featuring a diversity of voices behind the camera. If I've done my job, you won't just unlock the grammar of filmmaking – you'll be intrigued enough to explore films outside of your comfort zone. Sometimes, the greatest pleasures are discovered when investigating the unknown.

As you might imagine, *This Is How You Make a Movie* is not meant to be exhaustive but, rather, a tantalizing taste that will whet your artistic appetite. The real start to a film career involves going out and experimenting, but hopefully the tools laid out here will help set you on the right path. I've tried my best to summarize fundamental cinematic concepts into easy-to-understand little morsels. But you'll learn so much more once you grab that camera and create.

Tim Grierson

ACTING

Method

Drawing from personal experiences to deliver a searing, authentic performance

An entire book could be written about Method acting (or the Method), and so condensing this famous technique to just a few pages risks simplifying the process to such a degree as to be misleading. With that said, we'll defer to Alex Ates, a theater director and actor who wrote about the history and legacy of the Method for the acting publication *Backstage*, offering this thumbnail definition: "At its most simple, the Method is an internal, psychological technique that asserts an actor can train themselves, under regimented practice, to behave realistically under imaginary circumstances." In the same overview, he sought to correct a faulty assumption about what Method acting hopes to achieve, noting, "It does not encourage the crude reliving of experienced emotional events onstage. What [it] does promote is training to identify and consistently replicate the stimuli that could induce a similar rush and thrill to that of a lived moment."

In other words, the cultural cliché of Method actors drawing from some childhood trauma in order to be emotional isn't the point of this technique. Rather, Method actors are seeking naturalism in their performances, putting aside artifice for an accurate depiction of realistic behavior. Not every film calls for the Method, but its power is undeniable in the right setting.

Becoming a character

On the Waterfront
1954
Actor: Marlon Brando;
director: Elia Kazan

Marlon Brando is perhaps most associated with the Method. In his memoir *Songs My Mother Taught Me*, he discussed his time learning from famed acting teacher Stella Adler, writing that, "What Stella taught her students was how to discover the nature of their own emotional mechanics and therefore those of others. She taught me to be real and not to try to act out an emotion I didn't personally experience during a performance."

The Oscar-winning actor first demonstrated Method acting onstage, winning raves for his work in *A Streetcar Named Desire*. On-screen, he continued to deliver gritty, realistic portrayals. For 1954's *On the Waterfront*, he played Terry, a dockworker who once had dreams of being a boxer. As part of his preparation process, Brando spent some time with real dockworkers in order to learn how they did their job (he even loaded crates). Brando also trained in a boxing gym to get his footwork correct.

These behind-the-scenes tidbits aren't necessarily visible in *On the Waterfront*, but for Brando, they lent believability to his performance, giving the actor a guide for how to play this man. To become Terry, he had to understand his hobbies and occupation.

Diving into
the darkness

The King of Comedy
1982
Actors: Robert De Niro,
Jerry Lewis; director:
Martin Scorsese

Robert De Niro played the younger version of Marlon Brando's character in *The Godfather: Part II*, which is apt since the two men share an affinity for the Method. In his career, De Niro has undergone massive physical transformations – like the weight he put on to play Jake LaMotta in *Raging Bull* – but we're going to talk about his work in *The King of Comedy* to suggest other ways that the technique can be utilized.

This dark comedy about a mediocre, possibly deranged comic named Rupert Pupkin, who's obsessed with being discovered by talk-show legend Jerry Langford (Jerry Lewis), inspired De Niro to do plenty of research, including visiting comedy clubs and studying stand-ups' delivery. He also channeled Rupert's hostility in his day-to-day life during the shoot: Lewis famously invited De Niro to dinner, but De Niro responded, "I wanna blow your head off. How can we have dinner?"

That might be an extreme reaction, and De Niro's commitment to staying in character, if exhibited by another actor, might be incredibly off-putting. But the intensity of his performance as Rupert Pupkin is a marvel. And part of its secret was the actor's immersion into his character's dark psyche.

Staying connected

Lincoln
2012
Actors: Daniel Day-Lewis, Sally Field; director: Steven Spielberg

Daniel Day-Lewis is a giant of Method acting, immersing himself in his characters. But when discussing *Lincoln*, let's take a moment to consider his formidable costar, Sally Field, who plays the American president's wife, Mary Todd Lincoln. She, too, has been a student of the Method throughout her career. As she said around the film's release, "I've always worked like that, except that I had never felt like I had a place to sort of impose it on everybody else, mostly because I felt like they don't understand! I would be shy about letting anyone into my process, honestly – about telling them what I was doing. I would stay in [character] and go to my room or stay in my chair and do something that told everybody, 'Don't talk to me. Don't come near me.' I would totally stay in character as much as I could."

To prepare to play Mary Todd, the two-time Oscar-winner did extensive research into the woman's life. She and Day-Lewis exchanged texts, communicating as if writing letters to one another in the language of the period. And Field put on weight: "I went to a nutritionist, and I ate really the most god-awful stuff. It was repulsive. And after the end of every day, I felt like a pâté de foie gras goose."

Day-Lewis won Best Actor for his portrayal, which is far more dynamic, but Field brings the same amount of ferocity to her supporting role. It's a performance that's informed by a deep connection to Mary Todd both psychologically and physically. Field isn't as showy as her costar, but she's just as affecting.

Improvisation

Using the screenplay as a springboard to invent fresh, spontaneous reactions to a situation

In real life, we improvise all the time. Our evening plans get canceled, and so we have to decide what to do instead. We forget to pack something important for a road trip, and so we have to figure out how to live without it – or how to get another one. People are constantly operating on the fly, coming up with ideas on the spot.

When making movies, improvisation can also be crucial. Different filmmakers will use the technique in different ways, but it tends to be more of a tool in comedy. Loosely speaking, improvisation is when the actors disregard the script's dialogue, instead hatching lines and situations on set while the cameras roll. In the wrong hands, such a strategy could be disastrous. We'll look at three examples where improv helped a movie reach greater heights.

Building from an idea

This Is Spinal Tap
1984
Actors: Rob Reiner,
Christopher Guest;
director: Rob Reiner

When director Rob Reiner and actors Christopher Guest, Michael McKean and Harry Shearer began developing the idea of a pseudo-documentary concerning a woefully inept metal band named Spinal Tap, they didn't write a conventional screenplay. Instead, an outline was created that laid out the bare bones of the plot, as well as the characters' backstories. In place of scripted scenes, the cast ad-libbed their dialogue, working from the preexisting narrative spine so that they had some sense of direction about what needed to occur.

In the process, *This Is Spinal Tap* helped give birth to the "mockumentary" format, in which filmmakers create the illusion that we're watching a nonfiction film. A key component of this subgenre is actors who improvise (or seemingly improvise) their lines in order to seem more lifelike.

In a 2006 interview, Guest, who has gone on to direct several mockumentaries, including *Waiting for Guffman*, talked about the power of improv. "You're always caught off guard," he said. "That's the whole point. But it's not a free-for-all. It's very rigid in its preparation."

Leaving room for new ideas

Knocked Up
2007
Actors: Seth Rogen,
Katherine Heigl;
director: Judd Apatow

In modern comedy, few filmmakers have been more celebrated than Judd Apatow. And in movies like *Knocked Up*, the writer–director has incorporated improvisation, drawing from previous directors who used the technique as part of their on-set strategy. "When I started paying attention to movies, I discovered Barry Levinson," Apatow once said. "I loved his use of loose performance and some improvisation. *Diner* might have been one of the most influential movies on me when I was young."

Apatow balances scripted dialogue with moments of pure improvisation, encouraging his ensemble to riff off one another in order to come up with lively, believable, funny exchanges. Tim Bagley, an actor who's appeared in a few Apatow films, including *Knocked Up*, explained how the filmmaker achieves his effects. "He starts with a brilliantly written screenplay," Bagley said in 2012. "He uses it as a solid foundation. On the day, he shoots the draft of the scene he's written. Then he likes to rewrite and collaborate while the scene is on its feet being performed. He pitches a lot of lines, often while the camera is still rolling. He gives the actors several takes to improvise and play, allowing something inspired to happen in the moment. He gathers multiple options for when he's editing."

Letting the actor find the best moments

Girls Trip
2017
Actor: Tiffany Haddish;
director: Malcolm D. Lee

Tiffany Haddish has emerged as one of Hollywood's brightest new comedy stars, in large part thanks to her scene-stealing turn in 2017's *Girls Trip*, where she plays the wild card Dina, who leads her friends into increasingly crazy exploits. Many of her best lines were improvised, as director Malcolm D. Lee gave her the space to try different ideas. ("When we did *Girls Trip*, it was a lot of hours and a lot of takes," Haddish would later say.)

But despite Haddish's go-for-broke performance, which emphasizes how assertive and sexually confident her character is, Lee insisted Dina remain in the realm of believability. "I want these characters to be relatable no matter how silly or crazy they get," the director said around *Girls Trip*'s release. "There's a human connection – there's a vulnerability underneath Dina's craziness. There's more going on than what's on the surface."

That's an important reminder about improvisation. Giving actors the freedom to find their characters, and the best punch lines, can reap huge rewards. But it's also crucial to ensure that there's some sort of grounding – whether in the form of an outline, a screenplay or a desire to keep the characters relatable. Even when you're ad-libbing, it has to be connected to some kind of reality.

Rehearsal

Working on a story at the script stage, developing characters by reacting off the rest of the ensemble

Practice makes perfect. That adage is particularly true in cinema if you're working on a film that has the time and resources available to rehearse before shooting begins.

Rehearsals take many forms on a production. Stunt teams rehearse their elaborate, potentially dangerous action sequences extensively to ensure everyone's safety. But for this book, we're referring specifically to the rehearsal process that goes on between the director and the actors as they read through the screenplay to find the story's emotional and dramatic beats.

Perhaps the best-known rehearsal is the initial "table read" (or "read-through"), when the cast, the director, the writer(s) and possibly others (including producers) read the entire script aloud to get a sense of the narrative's scope, challenges, strengths and areas for improvement. While some actors and directors would rather not rehearse, preferring the spontaneity of being on set with the camera rolling, the process can allow an ensemble to get a feel for one another and develop chemistry between characters. A rehearsal primes everyone for the actual production.

Building rapport

Secrets & Lies
1996
Actors: Marianne
Jean-Baptiste,
Brenda Blethyn;
director: Mike Leigh

For Oscar-nominated writer–director Mike Leigh, rehearsal is the beginning of the creative journey to making a film. The superb *Secrets & Lies*, about a Black Londoner (Marianne Jean-Baptiste) who decides to seek out her birth mother, discovering to her surprise that it's a white woman (Brenda Blethyn), demonstrates how Leigh works with his cast to flesh out themes and characters, and eventually plot.

"There are people close to me who have [had] adoption-related experiences," he explained at the 1996 New York Film Festival. "And so I wanted for years to make a film which explored this predicament in a fictitious way. I also wanted to make a film about the new generation of young Black people who are moving on and getting away from the ghetto stereotypes. And these were jumping-off points for a film which turns out to be an exploration of roots and identity."

But Leigh doesn't start with a script. Instead, he brings in actors, engaging them in conversation about people they know in order to start building a character. Once Leigh settles on the character, he asks the actor to go deeper. "It made me realize how lazy I'd been before," Blethyn later told *The Guardian*. "I loved the experience of creating this character, getting under her skin. It's not just a question of learning the lines and saying them in the right order. You have to know how the person's feeling at the top of page one."

Such exacting preparation might seem outlandish, but for Leigh, the slow cultivation of the characters – even before a word is written on the page – allows for the rich, lifelike quality of his movies.

Finding a framework

Henry V
1989
Actors: Emma Thompson,
Kenneth Branagh;
director: Kenneth Branagh

Most people are familiar with William Shakespeare's work. But that doesn't mean different productions will put on the same staging of, say, *Hamlet*. The actors, the present circumstances, the locale and the director's particular ambitions will inform how the Bard's material will be interpreted.

Kenneth Branagh, who has directed several big-screen Shakespeare adaptations, can speak to the importance of rehearsal as a way to understand exactly how to attack the work. In a 1998 interview, he discussed some of the challenges, and how rehearsing can allow for conversations about how to play well-known characters and tap into the playwright's universal themes.

As Branagh put it, "If you're doing something like *Henry V*, for instance, it's useful to talk about the concept of honor as understood by people of the time, to talk about the concept of a Christian king, to bring this into rehearsal for the sake of the actors' imaginations, so that sometimes they can understand the real, direct import of things that otherwise may seem to emerge more casually from the play for us."

Rehearsal isn't just about memorizing lines; it is, in essence, a process to ensure that the entire creative team is on the same page and understands the material's underlying ideas. Even in the case of Shakespeare, a production has to be sure it knows what *its* specific take on a classic will be.

Testing commitment

Everybody Wants Some!!
2016
Actor: Juston Street (right);
director: Richard Linklater

Richard Linklater believes in preparing before a shoot. In a 2018 interview, the filmmaker said, "With actors, it starts with talking with them about their character, letting them explore the character, and then preparing with three weeks of rehearsal, which I think is essential."

For his bittersweet college-baseball comedy *Everybody Wants Some!!*, Linklater asked those who auditioned to tape themselves doing something athletic. For him, it was a way to see who would be up for the challenge of believably playing baseball players. In the same interview, Linklater recalled that some actors "[didn't] take the assignment seriously. I'm thinking, 'OK, if they do that, are they going to want to rehearse for three weeks and take this as more than just a job?' It has to be something fun that they really want to do."

Linklater views rehearsal as a way to gauge his actors' commitment to the material, as much as it is a chance to play and explore. "I find my movie in the writing and rehearsing, and the shooting is the final phase," he said. "My movies may have this looseness, but they're not loose. They're done. Because I'm big on prep, and rehearsals. I never do reshoots."

Monologue

Revealing a character's state of mind through his own words

As in real life, moviegoers don't prefer sitting through long, boring speeches. In everyday conversation, your long-winded friend can be incredibly tedious, so filmmakers have to be careful that they don't have their characters just talk endlessly. But when a person has something important to say – something that will require a little time (and patience) on the listener's part – the results can be intensely moving and dramatic. Used judiciously, a monologue can be a verbal powerhouse.

The monologue wasn't a creation of the movies. William Shakespeare wrote a few terrific ones in his day. But as with theater, cinema is adept at allowing a solitary individual to speak from the heart, the words serving several potential purposes. The monologue can reveal the character's worldview. It can underline the film's central themes. It can tell a colorful story whose point might be tied to something that happens in the movie. It can shine new light on an event or a character. Ideally, a monologue furthers the screenplay's dramatic or comedic elements. And most importantly, it should leave you spellbound, as the actor delivering the monologue takes center stage.

Righteousness

JFK
1991
Actor: Kevin Costner;
director: Oliver Stone

Legal thrillers are famous for their monologues: Court cases typically make time for lawyers to give closing arguments, and in movies those are often in the form of poetic summations of the film's key ideas. Near the end of *JFK*, which is about District Attorney Jim Garrison's (Kevin Costner) dogged pursuit of the truth behind the killing of President John F. Kennedy, we get a monologue that goes beyond an attorney providing an overview of his case – it's quite simply a treatise on how a politician's assassination reshaped a country.

At first, Costner speaks in a rather reserved manner, but as Garrison recounts the evidence pointing to a conspiracy that brought down the American president, his anger rises. The actor taps into the character's righteous indignation, but he also gets choked up, an indication of how personally affected Garrison was by Kennedy's murder. Through this monologue, director and cowriter Oliver Stone reveals aspects of his main character – his decency and his unbending belief that a horrible injustice has been committed. Garrison doesn't just speak for himself; his words underline Stone's own feelings about America's loss of innocence in the wake of this killing.

Movingly performed, Garrison's speech is the culmination of everything he's done throughout *JFK*, tilting at windmills and fighting a political system that wishes to silence him. The monologue's poignancy stems from the futility of his passionate quest.

Incitement

Glengarry Glen Ross
1992
Actor: Alec Baldwin;
director: James Foley

When David Mamet's Pulitzer Prize-winning play came to the big screen, the writer created a new scene early on to establish the stakes for the story's luckless salesmen (including Ed Harris, Jack Lemmon and Alan Arkin). Blake (Alec Baldwin), a representative from Premiere Properties, comes down to the office to tell them they have to produce results, or they're fired.

Blake's speech is a wonder of unfiltered machismo: He berates the employees, questions their masculinity and brags about his wealth and success. Baldwin performs the monologue with a swaggering confidence meant to assert his superiority and bully the salesmen into doing a better job. This is the only scene in which Blake appears, but the rest of *Glengarry Glen Ross* is infused by his inciting words. If these salesmen don't succeed, there's no mercy from their bosses – Blake has made that clear. In just a few minutes of screen time, Mamet gives us a potent, unforgettable character. We don't know a lot about Blake, but in his dazzlingly abusive speech, we learn enough.

Stupidity

National Lampoon's
Animal House
1978
Actors: Tom Hulce,
John Belushi; director:
John Landis

Many of the most famous movie monologues come from dramas, which might suggest that speeches always need to be about serious subjects. But take a look at *Animal House*, the anti-conformist 1970s comedy about a group of frat guys taking on the status quo. John Belushi plays Bluto, a drunken, slovenly member of Delta Tau Chi who isn't smart or noble, but when he starts talking, he's not going to let anything stop him.

Near the end of *Animal House*, it looks like Delta Tau Chi is going to be shut down. But while his fellow brothers are inconsolable, Bluto takes it upon himself to deliver a rousing speech to get them fired up. Sports films often have such monologues, which are meant to be stirring and inspirational. Instead, Bluto just starts blathering. "Nothing is over until we decide it is! Was it over when the Germans bombed Pearl Harbor? Hell, no!" Never mind that Bluto has none of his facts right – it was the Japanese who bombed Pearl Harbor. The whole point is that he's trying to encourage his brothers not to give up.

This monologue could only be delivered by Bluto, who's a lovable buffoon, and it's very much in keeping with the style of irreverent comedy that made *Animal House* a classic. Sometimes, being fired up is more important than knowing exactly what you want to say. It's a good reminder to all writers that a terrific movie speech doesn't have to feel scripted or elegant – enthusiasm counts, too.

Motivation

Understanding what drives your character, even if those reasons are elusive to everyone else

"What's my motivation?" Watch any movie or television program that's mocking pretentious actors, and it's a safe bet that one of the artsy characters will utter that line. For those who don't appreciate the skill that goes into performing, an actor's need for motivation might seem baffling, even ridiculous: *Just read the lines and play the part – how hard is that?* But such a simplistic interpretation of what goes into acting, besides being insulting, is deeply ill-informed.

When we talk about an actor's motivation, we're speaking of what drives his character to do what he does. Often, the motivation is obvious: He wants to rescue the damsel or win the big game or save the universe. But sometimes, a character's intentions are murkier, leaving the audience to ponder precisely what is prompting this person to go about his plan.

In these cases, it's up to the actor to make us believe the character's actions – even if we don't agree with his choices. Suddenly, this issue of "motivation" doesn't seem so academic. Indeed, it's essential for crafting a connection between the audience and an enigmatic, potentially morally slippery main character.

Finding the core of an unlovable character

Good Time
2017
Actor: Robert Pattinson;
directors: Benny and
Josh Safdie

This grungy New York thriller features a disreputable protagonist who drags us along on his strange journey. Directors Benny and Josh Safdie follow Connie (Robert Pattinson), a two-bit crook, after a bank heist goes bad. Connie's brother Nick (Benny Safdie) is picked up by the police, while Connie escapes, quickly trying to figure out how to raise bond money to secure Nick's release. When those efforts fail, Connie resorts to a more desperate plan – breaking his brother out of the hospital where he's been sent after a jailhouse altercation – but things soon go from bad to worse.

Not only is Connie a thief, but he's also a liar and self-centered, only thinking of himself and manipulating others in order to free Nick. On paper, this is a character who would be hard to root for. And yet, Pattinson makes him compelling. No one would describe Connie as "lovable," but the actor burrows inside him in such a way that this small-time hood has an internal logic that makes sense.

"He's just playing the hand that's dealt to him," Pattinson once told me. "I don't think he thinks he's dumb at all – he's someone who has philosophical ideas about things, but has absolutely no idea that even the concept of philosophy exists. He essentially thinks he's a genius [even if he's] just kind of relatively uninformed about things. I think he's just so focused on the end result that it just seems [to him] that things should be a certain way – he almost wills them into existence." Through these motivations, Pattinson was able to fashion an arresting character.

Forging a connection

Lost in Translation
2003
Actors: Scarlett
Johansson, Bill Murray;
director: Sofia Coppola

Filmmaker Sofia Coppola often scripts enigmatic characters whose motivations aren't quite clear. Her most acclaimed film, *Lost in Translation*, develops this idea through the story of Bob (Bill Murray), a washed-up actor, and Charlotte (Scarlett Johansson), a young woman he meets in Tokyo. He's there to film a commercial, she's killing time as her husband works on a photo shoot. Even though they couldn't be more different – he's famous and in middle age, while she's young and directionless – they're both battling disillusionment. They forge a connection with each other, although the movie never nails down how they feel about one another.

Coppola, who won an Oscar for her screenplay, once said of her inspiration for the story, "For everyone, there are those moments when you have great days with someone you wouldn't expect to. Then you have to go back to your real lives, but it makes an impression on you. It's what makes it so great and enjoyable. ... Sometimes with strangers, you can tell them something that you couldn't tell someone you know. But I just liked those brief moments of connection when they're feeling so disconnected. ... I've had friends like that where you have a flirtation but you're just friends. I wanted it to be more innocent. If they slept together, that would bring in reality."

To play these roles, Murray and Johansson had to walk a fine line. *Lost in Translation* isn't a romance, but it is a kind of love story about lost souls finding something in one another. The actors had to depict that ambiguity, resisting the urge to make the characters' connection more traditionally passionate. They're motivated not by sexual attraction but, rather, something more profound and ineffable.

Understanding a monster's inner pain

Precious
2009
Actor: Mo'Nique;
director: Lee Daniels

Mo'Nique garnered universal acclaim (and a Best Supporting Actress Oscar) for her role as Mary, an unrepentant monster who sexually and verbally abuses her daughter Precious (Gabourey Sidibe). But for Mo'Nique, understanding the character meant tapping into the abuse she herself faced as a girl.

"I was molested by my older brother," she told *Essence*. "And even when I confronted him and told my parents, he said I was lying, and nothing was really done ... I'm not blaming my parents because me and my brother were both their children, and I just don't know the kind of position they felt they were in ... I'll never forget my mother saying, 'If it's true, it will surface again,' and I remember thinking, 'Why would I lie? Why is there even an *if* in this?'"

To be clear, we are not suggesting that such pointed personal trauma is required to craft a performance as wrenching as Mo'Nique gave in *Precious*. But she believed playing Mary was, in some small way, an opportunity to shed light on abuse. "It's my obligation to let people know," she said, "and to tell them to watch their children."

Non-professionals

Casting everyday people to bring realism to a film

There's always been something slightly demeaning about calling people who aren't actors "non-professionals" or even "non-actors." (Even referring to them as "everyday people" seems a bit snotty.) Although acting is a serious craft that talented men and women devote their lives to perfecting, it's not as if non-professionals are so lacking the basic understanding of conveying emotion that they're somehow inferior life forms.

So, with that caveat acknowledged, let's note that directors will sometimes cast non-professional actors for crucial roles in their films precisely because they're seeking a performer who doesn't have the traditional training. We will encounter some of the most famous instances of this kind of casting later on (for example *Bicycle Thieves*; see page 175), and usually the choice is made to add realism to the story. Sometimes, though, it's because the real person can play the character far better than even the greatest actor could.

Creating
anonymity

Elephant
2003
Actors: Alicia Miles,
John Robinson;
director: Gus Van Sant

Elephant, which won the Palme d'Or at the Cannes Film Festival, was a response to the 1999 shooting at Columbine High School in Colorado, which killed thirteen and shocked the nation. But rather than enlisting recognizable stars to play the teen characters, director Gus Van Sant decided to cast many non-professionals.

His strategy wasn't surprising. One of the key reasons to use non-pros is to bypass one of the few downsides to working with movie stars – which is that, because they're so famous, high-profile actors have established a relationship with the audience where we know them from dozens of other roles. It can be harder to accept, say, Will Smith as an average, ordinary person – we keep remembering, "Hey, that's Will Smith." By comparison, non-actors have no history with the viewer. As far as we're concerned, they're a blank slate.

This approach is valuable in a movie like *Elephant*, which turns the Columbine tragedy into an anonymous school shooting that could happen anywhere. And because we don't recognize Van Sant's actors, we're more inclined to accept the scenario as commonplace, universal, nondescript. Even though *Elephant* is a work of fiction, its non-professional cast gives it an air of unpolished reality. In this way, Van Sant steps away from the specific details of Columbine to speak to something far larger and more troublesome in our society – the isolation, helplessness and anger that allow such tragedies to occur.

Being in the moment

Fish Tank
2009
Actor: Katie Jarvis;
director: Andrea Arnold

Filmmaker Andrea Arnold will sometimes cast non-professionals as her leads. In a 2016 interview, she explained why that can be her preference. "Sometimes, I think [professional] actors want lots of things to hang on to, and I completely understand that," she said. "[But] I don't rehearse – I don't give them the script at the beginning. I kind of like the idea that they have to be in the moment and there's not a lot to hang on to."

When she made her 2009 coming-of-age drama *Fish Tank*, she went with a non-pro, Katie Jarvis, to play Mia, a directionless, impoverished teenager who begins to have feelings for her mom's boyfriend (Michael Fassbender). "They're being themselves," Arnold said of her non-professional actors, "but they're being themselves within a certain universe. ... With Katie, I was constantly asking her to be herself, but at the same time, I'm getting her to state my words. She's wearing clothes that I've given her. I'm giving her certain scenarios that she would never normally be in. She's going through something that I've created, but she's going through it as herself."

Reliving a personal experience

Close-Up
1990
Cast: Mohsen Makhmalbaf, Hossain Sabzian; director: Abbas Kiarostami

The late Iranian writer–director Abbas Kiarostami often played with our perception of reality. Perhaps his finest example of this was in *Close-Up*, which brilliantly blurs the line between fiction and nonfiction. It is, in essence, a recreation of actual events that are performed by the individuals who were part of those events.

Close-Up concerns a film lover named Hossain Sabzian who passes himself off as Mohsen Makhmalbaf, a well-known Iranian director, in order to ingratiate himself with a well-to-do family, who happily provide their home for what he claims will be his next movie. Sabzian went on trial for his deception, which inspired Kiarostami to make a film about the situation and its repercussions.

Kiarostami convinced the participants to play themselves, which creates a strange sensation as we watch *Close-Up*. Are we watching the "real" people? Are they "acting"? How does the recreation of actual events change the truth of those events? The filmmaker's bold gambit simply wouldn't have been as fascinating if he had recruited professional actors to play these roles. It's crucial that we see the actual men so that we can investigate how we all try to rewrite and reframe the past – and how we often blindly accept the concept of "reality" in film.

DIRECTING

Framing

Determining the geography of a scene by where you place the actors

Characters don't just speak dialogue back and forth to each other. A good director also thinks about how a scene is staged, which encompasses many factors. Here, we'll pay attention to what's called framing. Stated simply, this is the process by which a director determines where the actors will be positioned in the scene and how they'll move through the frame. These creative decisions, often made in concert with camera and lighting considerations, are collectively known as blocking.

When done well, most viewers won't think too much about the framing of a scene. Instead, we just focus on the drama that's unfolding before us. With this in mind, let's look at three seemingly straightforward scenes and examine what's going on in the framing, and what it's trying to communicate.

An unrequited love

Do the Right Thing
1989
Director: Spike Lee;
cinematography:
Ernest Dickerson; actors:
Ruby Dee, Ossie Davis

Spike Lee's powerful *Do the Right Thing* dissects race and class in America, using as its crucible one New York City block on an extremely hot summer day. There are several central characters in this Oscar-nominated film but, for a moment, let's turn our attention to two peripheral players, who have their own mini-drama playing out.

Ruby Dee plays Mother Sister, who sits at her window and surveys the action going on around her. Occasionally, she's pestered by Da Mayor (Ossie Davis), a drunkard who tries to woo her, very unsuccessfully. The above still illustrates, wordlessly, their dynamic. Even if you've never seen *Do the Right Thing*, this image tells you everything you need to know about their personalities.

Note Mother Sister's disinterested look, and how she observes Da Mayor out of the corner of her eye and over her shoulder. Her body isn't turned toward him, and her hands are clenched and pointed away. There's nothing about her posture that suggests she's pleased by Da Mayor's advances. In addition, observe how she's framed by her open window, which creates a protective box that further separates her from him.

By comparison, Da Mayor leans into the frame, his posture far more apprehensive and pleading. The way Lee blocks the scene, Da Mayor is practically an intruder, which is how Mother Sister feels about this man. He's reaching out to her, while she sits in her power position. Neither character has said a word, but we understand the underlying tension perfectly.

A pair of rivals

A Dangerous Method
2011
Director: David
Cronenberg;
cinematography:
Peter Suschitzky; actors:
Michael Fassbender,
Viggo Mortensen

A Dangerous Method tells the true story of the uneasy professional relationship between Sigmund Freud (Viggo Mortensen) and Carl Jung (Michael Fassbender). Jung looked up to Freud, who served as a prickly mentor to the younger man, and the film's dialogue features plenty of instances in which these two towering figures of psychoanalysis debate their differing perspectives. But how do you visualize discord?

The above still suggests a few ways. David Cronenberg places Freud in the foreground, his striking countenance dominating the frame, which implies he's the intellectual superior of his friend. And notice that Jung is smaller, seemingly reacting to Freud, who's the more powerful. However, both characters are in focus, a way for the filmmaker to indicate that A Dangerous Method is a battle between two mighty minds. That tension is only underlined by the taut way that Jung holds his cup. This is not an image of two close comrades. There's a silent battle going on in this snapshot, and in the film itself.

A close embrace

Let the Sunshine In
2017
Director: Claire Denis;
cinematography: Agnès
Godard; actors: Paul
Blain, Juliette Binoche

In *Let the Sunshine In*, Juliette Binoche plays Isabelle, a middle-aged artist struggling to find true love. She has a few men jockeying for her affections, but none of them seems ideal. Then, in one remarkable scene, she's swept off her feet by a stranger who slow-dances with her at a club. Is the scene real or imagined? The beauty of the moment, and the way director Claire Denis shoots it, is that we're never quite sure.

The blocking of such a scene can be tricky: How does one capture the uncertainty about whether it's real or fantasy? Let's look at this image, which is a nice illustration of the sequence's effect.

Denis has the two actors close together, with Binoche's eyes closed, as if she's in a dream. Because we don't see the man's face, the still suggests that he's not as important as Isabelle is. It's not simply that *Let the Sunshine In* is her movie – this is *her* scene, and so our attention is riveted on her reaction.

In addition, the two characters are in the corner of the frame, cut off from everyone else (and maybe the real world). We feel like we're eavesdropping on a private, delicate moment. The way Isabelle holds on to him with just one arm underlines the fragility of this encounter. Denis communicates all these emotions with her subtle blocking.

Depth of Field

Strategizing how much of the frame you want in focus

When a filmmaker is determining the depth of field in a shot, she's not just thinking about what she wants in focus, but why. The easiest way to describe "depth of field" is that it's a measurement of the area of the frame in which objects are in focus. So, for instance, a shot with shallow depth of field has very little focus area in it (in these shots, the principal subject is in focus, but everything in front of and behind him would be blurry). The greater depth of field, the wider the focus area is. (On a technical level, the greater your lens's aperture, the more your depth of field will shrink. Likewise, a longer lens will diminish your depth of field.)

These camera adjustments might not seem that important: After all, as long as your main character can be seen easily, what does it matter what happens in the background? Let's see how depth of field can add drama to a scene.

Alienation

Moonlight
2016
Director: Barry Jenkins;
cinematography:
James Laxton; actor:
Alex Hibbert

The Oscar-winning *Moonlight* is the story of a young, gay, Black man strug-gling to find himself. Director and cowriter Barry Jenkins articulates Chiron's internal anguish in plenty of ways, but this simple shot says more than reams of dialogue could.

In this image, taken from the first chapter of *Moonlight*'s triptych of tales, we see Chiron as a child (played by Alex Hibbert) as he begins to suspect that he's gay. Confusion over his sexual identity is only one of his anxieties, though: His mother is battling drug addiction, and he doesn't have any strong male role models in his life, save for a local dealer who befriends him.

What this still evokes so powerfully is Chiron's sense of alienation. And much of that feeling comes from the shallow depth of field. Chiron is in sharp focus, but the world around him is blurry. He's cut off from his surroundings, almost as if he's in his own world. If you want to spiritually isolate your character, consider a shallow depth of field.

Complexity

The Maltese Falcon
1941
Director: John Huston;
cinematography: Arthur
Edeson; actors: Humphrey
Bogart, Mary Astor,
Barton MacLane, Peter
Lorre, Ward Bond

The film most associated with deep-focus photography is *Citizen Kane*, and indeed the use of the technique in that film is discussed later in this book (see page 87). But the Orson Welles classic isn't alone in incorporating a wide depth of field – it's not even the only movie from 1941 to do so.

The Maltese Falcon follows hard-boiled private eye Sam Spade (Humphrey Bogart) as he tries to help a beautiful stranger, Ruth Wonderly (Mary Astor), locate her missing sister. Writer–director John Huston puts Spade through a series of twists and turns, and he wants us to see everything in every scene.

As this image demonstrates, the entire frame remains in sharp focus. As a result, *The Maltese Falcon* is a film noir in which we're invited to consider all the clues and all the characters Spade encounters as possible leads into the woman's disappearance. There's a complexity to the film that comes across because of the wide depth of field, lending the proceedings an almost novelistic quality – which is appropriate, after all, since the source material was Dashiell Hammett's 1930 novel.

Rebirth

Apocalypse Now
1979
Director: Francis
Ford Coppola;
cinematography:
Vittorio Storaro;
actor: Martin Sheen

A hallucinatory war film, *Apocalypse Now* stars Martin Sheen as Willard, a US soldier assigned to kill Kurtz (Marlon Brando), a brilliant tactician who's gone rogue during the Vietnam War. Willard isn't sure he'll be able to execute his orders, but once he finally meets the legendary warrior at the end of the film, he goes through with his murderous mission.

To help illustrate the personal transformation that Willard has undergone by killing Kurtz, director Francis Ford Coppola keeps his protagonist in vivid focus, while his surroundings blur out. Visually, we understand that this disillusioned soldier isn't the same man he was at the beginning of this journey – he now stands apart from the environment around him. Indeed, there may no longer be a place in the world for a man like Willard, who has seen the horrors of war up close. Everyday life may simply be too strange for him now.

Bear in mind, none of this is communicated through dialogue. Instead, we *feel* it from the shallow depth of field.

Tracking Shot

Following along with your characters as they navigate through a space, which creates a sense of energy and movement in your film

Movies embed us with their main characters. We're by their side, often literally, as they navigate through the story's obstacles and twists. A tracking shot (or a oner) can be an effective tool for cementing a viewer's relationship with your protagonist. It's a camera move in which we follow along with an actor (or group of actors) through a space. Because there's no cut, a tracking shot gives us a sense of effort being exerted – both by the camera and the character – to complete an action. The technique can also illustrate the scope of the character's surroundings or the perilousness of his situation. It's a camera move that suggests energy and drama.

In recent years, digital trickery has allowed for some seemingly seamless tracking shots to, in fact, be a stitched-together collection of separate shots (Alfonso Cuarón used this trick magnificently in *Children of Men*). We don't consider that "cheating" by any stretch of the imagination. What matters is that your tracking shot conveys emotionally and narratively what you want to get across as a storyteller.

The madness of war

Atonement
2007
Director: Joe Wright;
cinematography:
Seamus McGarvey;
actor: James McAvoy

James McAvoy plays Robbie, whose love affair with Cecilia (Keira Knightley) is undercut by a third party's deception. As a result, his life goes in a very different direction, eventually finding himself fighting in World War II during the battle of Dunkirk. *Atonement* takes us to those bloody beaches through a deft tracking shot.

The scene was photographed by camera operator Peter Robertson, who shot with a Steadicam. In an interview with *Variety* at the time, he said, "I have to be inspired by the shot, because I'm the first person, before even the audience, who has to see and make the shot work. It was an idea that challenged the gods, but once we got used to the idea, I said, 'We're going for this, and it's going to look great.'"

Indeed, the sequence is complicated logistically, involving everything from horses being shot to a random soldier performing a routine on a pommel horse, but the camera keeps an eye on Robbie throughout. We watch as he walks through the surreal environment, taking in all the strange sights around him, and the longer the tracking shot goes on, the more bewildering the tableau becomes. Plus, we get a sense of the scale and horror of this particular battle. Robbie is our guide – the camera heroically tries to keep up as he moves ever forward through this nightmarish landscape.

The battle
to stay alive

Children of Men
2006
Director: Alfonso
Cuarón; cinematography:
Emmanuel Lubezki;
actors: Clive Owen,
Clare-Hope Ashitey

The twenty-first century has given us several indelible dystopian dramas, but *Children of Men* may be the bleakest. In its depiction of a near-future society without hope – and, seemingly, without the ability to reproduce anymore – the film immerses us in a desperate situation.

And yet, director Alfonso Cuarón fills the screen with such wondrous sequences that it's exhilarating to watch this otherwise dour tale. He's especially adept at tracking shots, incorporating them a few times during the story. One of the most memorable involves the reluctant hero Theo (Clive Owen) trying to escort a young pregnant woman, Kee (Clare-Hope Ashitey), to safety. Suddenly, he finds himself in the middle of a war zone, dodging bullets and frantically on the run.

In the sequence, Cuarón sends Owen from street level to a nearby building. The thrill of the scene's choreography is palpable as we legitimately feel like all hell is breaking loose around our protagonist. But the tracking shot also under-lines Theo and Kee's fragility. The camera movements aren't smooth, almost mimicking the footage shot by war photographers. We know that these characters have been through something horrifying because we feel like *we* have, too.

The agony
of a struggle

The Turin Horse
2011
Directors: Béla Tarr
and Ágnes Hranitzky;
cinematography: Fred
Kelemen; actor: Erika Bók

The Turin Horse is a symphony of long takes, a specialty of Hungarian auteur Béla Tarr. In the film, an elderly farmer (János Derzsi) and his adult daughter (Erika Bók) live a difficult existence in the middle of nowhere, and Tarr and codirector Ágnes Hranitzky chronicle their misery in exacting detail with carefully composed shots.

Outside the family's cottage, the wind blows mercilessly, and in one of the film's most striking sequences, the daughter ventures out with a bucket, fighting the brutalizing gales to reach her destination. That may not seem very cinematic, but the elemental power of *The Turin Horse*'s imagery gives the deceptively simple scene a mythic force. And much of that is achieved because of the tracking shot, which highlights how much the daughter must struggle. The audience is right behind Bók, literally, as the actress executes this difficult action. We are not spared the character's anguish. In fact, we share in it.

Close-up

Focusing on the intimacy and emotion of the human face

"All right, Mr. DeMille, I'm ready for my close-up." That line, spoken by the deluded actress Norma Desmond (Gloria Swanson) near the end of *Sunset Boulevard*, is probably what most moviegoers think of when discussing the filmmaking technique of placing the camera close to an actor's face. A close-up allows a character to dominate the frame, giving us an intimate view of her expression and, in theory, a window into what she's thinking and feeling. It can be a sort of cinematic punctuation, the shot's immediacy serving as a startling contrast to the shots that came before. It can also strip an actor bare, exposing her to the audience with an emotional nakedness that can be powerful or uncomfortable. We're drawn in by a close-up – we cannot look away.

On a technical level, a close-up (as its name implies) is a shot that captures an image up close. Inanimate objects get close-ups as well if they have a metaphorical or narrative importance – think of the snow globe in Charles Foster Kane's hand in *Citizen Kane* – but for our purposes, we'll focus on the human face.

Emotion

Persona
1966
Director: Ingmar Bergman;
cinematography:
Sven Nykvist; actor:
Liv Ullmann

"The close-up, the correctly illuminated, directed and acted close-up of an actor, is and remains the height of cinematography," visionary Swedish auteur Ingmar Bergman once said. "There is nothing better. That incredibly strange and mysterious contact you can suddenly experience with another soul through an actor's gaze. A sudden thought, blood that drains away or blood that pumps into the face, the trembling nostrils, the suddenly shiny complexion or mute silence, that is to me some of the most incredible and fascinating moments you will ever experience."

It's little surprise that Bergman felt so passionately about the close-up. A chronicler of the human soul, the filmmaker spent his career excavating the psychic trauma lurking within his tormented characters. By placing the camera close to his actors' faces, he created an emotional landscape for us to study, and he elicited performances that were remarkably open.

In *Persona*, Bibi Andersson plays Alma, a nurse assigned to care for Elisabet (Liv Ullmann), an acclaimed actress who seems to have had a breakdown – without warning, she's stopped speaking. The two women spend some time together in a house away from the city so that Elisabet can recuperate, only to discover that their personalities are starting to merge.

Bergman makes extensive use of close-ups in *Persona* as he leaves us feeling uneasy about this difficult relationship between caregiver and performer. Staring intently at Andersson's and Ullmann's faces, his camera hints at their troubled interior lives. In Bergman's hands, the technique probes the minute facets of the human experience, underlining every sliver of anguish and apprehension in real time.

Starkness

The Passion of Joan of Arc
1928
Director: Carl Theodor
Dreyer; cinematography:
Rudolph Maté; actor:
Maria Falconetti

In *Sunset Boulevard*, Norma Desmond, who was a star during the silent era, laments this new age of talkies. "We didn't need dialogue," she sniffs. "We had faces!" A landmark silent film, *The Passion of Joan of Arc*, illustrates what Desmond meant.

The film chronicles Joan's (Maria Falconetti) final moments as she is tried for heresy, convicted and executed. Director Carl Theodor Dreyer aimed for utter realism in this story of the fifteenth-century martyr, drawing on extensive research to craft this portrait, and he relied on intense close-ups to make the audience feel that they were as close to the drama as possible.

The effect is devastating: In *The Passion of Joan of Arc*, there is no escape for the viewer, who experiences Joan's ordeal right alongside her. Falconetti's emotive face says more than dialogue ever could.

Romance

If Beale Street Could Talk
2018
Director: Barry Jenkins;
cinematography: James
Laxton; actors: KiKi
Layne, Stephan James

"It's important for the audience to have a direct connection to the character," director Barry Jenkins said in 2018, "and when an actor's performing, there's always some degree of distance. If the performance goes away, and there's this perfect fusion between actor and character, then I want the audience to look right into that person's eyes."

For his adaptation of the James Baldwin novel, Jenkins incorporated close-ups of his leads, KiKi Layne and Stephan James, who play young lovers who, occasionally, look directly at the camera. *If Beale Street Could Talk* is a film about the beauty and warmth of true love, and close-ups allow us to feel embedded in the characters' passion. It's an intimacy that's vulnerable but also intensely moving.

"I think when you think of chemistry, you think, 'Oh, those two actors just want to tear each other's clothes off,'" Jenkins said in the same interview. "And that's not what I'm speaking of when I speak of chemistry. I'm talking about two people who feel legitimately connected, whose viewpoints and thoughts dovetail." He achieves that effortlessly by drawing us close to these lovers.

Long Shot

Moving the camera back in order to get a better look

The master shot is the filming of a scene from beginning to end in one take, which is then supplemented by shots of individual moments or actors that can later be used by the editor to shape the sequence for maximum dramatic impact. Although it can be similar to a master shot, a long shot is any shot that captures the action of a scene from such a distance that the viewer can see the characters' entire bodies, as well as the environment around them.

In sports betting, a "long shot" is a competitor without much chance of winning. In movies, a long shot (also known as a wide shot) can be equally risky, but the best examples of the technique show us reality in a dazzling, unorthodox way. Plus, it can make for great visual humor.

Humor

City Lights
1931
Director: Charlie Chaplin;
cinematography: Roland
Totheroh and Gordon
Pollock; actors: Harry
Myers, Charlie Chaplin

"Life is a tragedy when seen in close-up, but a comedy in long shot." That quote is attributed to Charlie Chaplin, who knew a few things about comedy. One of Hollywood's first auteurs, who wrote, directed, produced and starred in his own movies, Chaplin innovatively worked in long shots so that we could fully appreciate his Tramp character's shenanigans. Because Chaplin was such a graceful silent-screen performer, filming himself up close would have lessened the humor. Only by moving the camera back could we get the full picture.

City Lights is a fine example of Chaplin's brilliance. Long shots capture the absurdity of his set pieces, and because the camera is set back, it creates a deadpan effect because the characters are small in the frame. Plus, a good long shot can satisfy our need to see the whole scene in one frame, watching how the Tramp interacts with those around him. There's a tricky choreography to Chaplin's physical comedy – why not savor it all in one shot?

Tension

Playtime
1967
Director: Jacques Tati;
cinematography:
Jean Badal and
Andréas Winding;
actor: Jacques Tati

The visually inventive comedy *Playtime* might seem bizarre to those unaware of the strategy that director–star Jacques Tati incorporates in his satire of modern life. The reason why viewers may be thrown off by *Playtime*'s look is that Tati does away with filmmaking conventions like the use of close-ups and reaction shots. Instead, he pulls his camera back so that we don't just see his main character, M. Hulot (played by Tati), but also the confusing, chaotic, cosmopolitan world of Paris. We see a man at war with his environment.

Tati constructed a massive set ("Tativille") for *Playtime*, in which Hulot unsuccessfully applies for a job at a maddeningly inefficient high-tech office building, spends some time with friends, and attends the blowout launch party for a chic new restaurant. In each of these sequences, we often see Hulot from the back or the side, and almost always at a distance. Tati crafted a comedy that emphasized the futility of the individual in an increasingly modernized metropolis. To communicate that point visually, it was important to diminish Hulot in the frame.

In theory, long shots should nullify the comedy or energy of a scene – after all, everything's too far away for us to get a strong sense of exactly what's happening, right? But here, the long shots allow for a fresh comedic perspective we don't normally get, like the famous scene in which Hulot looks down at a series of office cubicles, the workers zipping around like drones in a glass-and-steel hive.

Perspective

*Close Encounters of
the Third Kind*
1977
Director: Steven
Spielberg;
cinematography:
Vilmos Zsigmond

One of the great advantages of long shots is that they create a sense of perspective. If you want to illustrate how massive an object is, sometimes the best strategy is to pull the camera back, just so the audience can take in the size of what they're looking at.

Steven Spielberg's 1977 sci-fi drama imagines a scenario in which aliens come to Earth to make contact with the human race. Before we meet any extraterrestrials, however, Spielberg hints at the magnitude of this event by suggesting how large their ships are. Throughout *Close Encounters of the Third Kind*, we see glimpses of the ships, but it's only during the stupendous finale that we finally get a great view of these majestic vessels. And that requires the director to utilize long shots.

This still image is a fine example of the device's power. We understand how big the ship is because it's shown in relation to the tiny humans at the bottom of the frame. A long shot can be awe-inspiring, as *Close Encounters* so deftly illustrates.

Aspect Ratio

Deciding how wide the frame should be to maximize the drama

Filmmakers spend a lot of time considering what information needs to be in the frame, but they also have to ponder what kind of frame they want. A movie's aspect ratio determines how the image will be presented in the theater. With the emergence of IMAX and smartphones, we've become accustomed to images in drastically different formats. But even with conventional cinematic aspect ratios, directors face a wide variety of possibilities.

On one end of the spectrum, there's 4:3, which indicates the image's width in relation to its height. In other words, this is a rather boxy, squarelike frame, and it was used during the first decades of film (4:3 is so associated with old-time moviemaking that modern directors may switch to that format to suggest a silent film or that what we're seeing is archival). But 4:3 is still used for strategic reasons in contemporary film.

Two striking recent examples are *Meek's Cutoff* and *American Honey*. The former, directed by American independent filmmaker Kelly Reichardt, follows a collection of increasingly desperate characters navigating the Oregon Trail during the 1840s. *American Honey* is the brainchild of English writer–director Andrea Arnold, who chronicles a group of young people traveling across America in a van while trying to sell magazine subscriptions.

In both cases, a more traditional, wider aspect ratio would seem to make sense. *Meek's Cutoff* is ostensibly a Western, a genre that boasts sweeping landscapes and majestic outdoor imagery. Likewise, *American Honey* is a road movie, where the sprawling freeways would be well-suited to a less boxy aspect ratio. But Reichardt and Arnold intentionally subvert expectations. Their reasons prove provocative, while demonstrating how an aspect ratio can add thematic depth to a film.

Creating tension by shrinking the frame

Meek's Cutoff
2010
Director: Kelly Reichardt;
cinematography:
Chris Blauvelt; actor:
Michelle Williams

Reichardt was asked why she chose to shoot in 4:3 for *Meek's Cutoff*, which stars Michelle Williams as a pioneer who begins to doubt her scout's (Bruce Green-wood) ability to guide them to safety while traversing the desolate American desert. "I felt like the square [aspect ratio] gave you an idea of the closed view that the women have because of their bonnets," she told *Fresh Air*'s Terry Gross in 2011. "You'd be traveling in this big community where you'd never have privacy. But also, it's a really lonely journey. And I think cutting out the peripheral, it does leave you with the idea that something could be there that you don't know about – and so it offers that kind of tension."

Indeed, *Meek's Cutoff* is noticeably unsettling simply because we can't see the environment around the characters. There's a sense of claustrophobia: Even though Williams and her costars are in a vast desert, they feel trapped in their circumstance. The 4:3 aspect ratio removes the romantic notion of the Old West as a place of renewal and adventure. The characters are literally boxed in.

Using 4:3 to emphasize the individual

American Honey
2016
Director: Andrea Arnold;
cinematography: Robbie
Ryan; actors: Sasha Lane,
Shia LaBeouf

For Arnold, who has often shot in 4:3, the choice is more one of personal preference. When I interviewed her around the release of *American Honey* in 2016, she explained that her decision wasn't so much about going against the grain as it was in emphasizing what matters most to her. "My main reason for picking that ratio is that I feel like [4:3] frames a human being really beautifully," she told me. "My films are about human beings – I want the human being to have some power, and that [aspect] ratio gives the human frame power."

When you watch *American Honey* (or Arnold's other 4:3 films, like her treatment of *Wuthering Heights*), the characters are foregrounded in a way that makes us feel close to them and their experience. Sasha Lane made her big-screen debut as Star, a directionless young woman who finds her purpose when she hits the open road with fellow misfits and outcasts (including Shia LaBeouf's greasy Jake). Arnold's camera wants us to notice Star more than her surroundings. As a result, *American Honey* is one of the most intimate of road pictures.

Painting on a large canvas for maximum grandeur

Chinatown
1974
Director: Roman Polanski; cinematography: John A. Alonzo; actors: Faye Dunaway, Jack Nicholson

For a completely different approach, a filmmaker could opt to shoot in 2.35 (or, 2.35:1), which gives the image a wider, more horizontal look. One of the great uses of a widescreen aspect ratio is 1974's *Chinatown*. Director Roman Polanski and cinematographer John A. Alonzo present us with a sun-draped Los Angeles noir as cynical private investigator Jake Gittes (Jack Nicholson) is hired to spy on a rich woman's (Faye Dunaway) philandering husband, quickly realizing that something far more ominous is going on.

While *Meek's Cutoff* and *American Honey* cut off the frame so that we notice what's missing – or focus on what the director wants us to focus on – *Chinatown* has a doomed grandeur that seems to encompass the entire city. Gittes and the other characters become part of the fabric of Los Angeles – the surroundings are as significant as the individuals – and so the 2.35 aspect ratio hints at a world that's immense and untamed, a major American metropolis that's only starting to come into its own. Interestingly, *Chinatown* depicts its own kind of Wild West, and Gittes is its reluctant sheriff at odds with the greed and corruption swirling around him.

With all three movies, the aspect ratio might not be the first thing you notice, but it's a creative choice that impacts how we receive these films' narratives. The shape of the frame is as critical as what happens within it.

Forced Perspective

Utilizing an optical illusion to play with size and scope

We live in an age of wall-to-wall special effects. Computer-generated imagery (CGI) has completely revolutionized filmmaking. And yet, some old-school techniques still work very effectively. One of them is something called forced perspective, which utilizes an optical illusion to trick the viewer into perceiving something that isn't, in fact, on the screen.

In essence, the trick is achieved by placing objects at different distances from the camera but creating the illusion they reside on the same plane. Because a movie screen is only two-dimensional, we misjudge the sizes of those two objects, thinking one is bigger (or smaller) than it actually is. Because we don't have the proper perspective – or, rather, because we don't see the image in three dimensions – our mind creates a distorted perspective.

If that sounds confusing, a few real-world examples will illustrate how cunning forced perspective can be for an inventive filmmaker.

Little big men

Elf
2003
Director: Jon Favreau;
cinematography:
Greg Gardiner;
actor: Will Ferrell

In this Will Ferrell comedy, Buddy is a human being who, as a baby, accidentally ends up at the North Pole with Santa Claus and his diminutive elves. Thinking that he himself is an elf, Buddy keeps growing, but all his coworkers stay small, leading to plenty of amusing scenarios.

The challenge for director Jon Favreau, however, was to show that contrast in size without using digital effects. He went with forced perspective. In a 2013 interview with *Rolling Stone*, he explained how that worked. "The forced perspective is where you build two sets, one smaller than the other. ... One set is raised and closer and smaller, and one is bigger and further away," Favreau said. "And if you line up those two sets and measure them, you can have one person on one set appear to be much larger than a person on the other set."

The effect is seamless enough that we simply think that Buddy looms over his cast mates. But it's merely our perspective that is being manipulated.

Far away,
so close

Songs from the
Second Floor
2000
Director: Roy Andersson;
cinematography:
István Borbás and
Jesper Klevenås

Award-winning Swedish filmmaker Roy Andersson makes wry, deadpan comedies about sad people living in bleak times. The viewer never knows whether laughing or sighing is the proper response to the melancholic, odd tableaux he presents us in his single-shot scenes.

Part of his technique is constructing sets that distort our perception. He works with *trompe l'oeil*, which is a form of forced perspective that gives the impression of three dimensions, when in fact you're only seeing two. Take, as an example, this scene from *Songs from the Second Floor*. The room seems like it stretches off into the distance. In reality, the background is far closer to the camera than that – it's simply that, because the objects in the back are smaller, we believe they're further away.

"I've come to realize that I can't shoot real environments. I prefer a hyper-reality," Andersson said in 2014. "[My set] looks real but it's purified and condensed. I'm fascinated by how life's grandness, smallness and mortality appear much clearer this way."

Up, up
and away

King Kong
1933
Directors: Merian C.
Cooper and Ernest
B. Schoedsack;
cinematography:
Eddie Linden, Vernon
Walker and J.O. Taylor

King Kong was one of the first films to make extensive use of special effects, including incorporating stop-motion to bring the titular beast to life. Forced perspective was a tool implemented by directors Merian C. Cooper and Ernest B. Schoedsack, particularly during the stirring finale when Kong breaks free in New York City and does battle with planes atop the Empire State Building.

In his book *King Kong: The History of a Movie Icon from Fay Wray to Peter Jackson*, author and script analyst Ray Morton provides some background on how the achievement was accomplished. "The airplanes were a mix of the real planes shot by Schoedsack and the miniature planes animated by [effects artist Willis H.] O'Brien and his team," Morton writes. "The planes were built in several sizes, with the smaller ones placed in the backgrounds of the shots to create a forced perspective impression that they were farther away than they actually were."

Generations later, *King Kong* still holds up as a marvelous example of special-effects cinema. The use of forced perspective helps give the film's climax its electric jolt.

Canted Angle

Tilting the camera, heightening the tension

We take for granted that the images we see in real life are level. Because we stand up straight, our head not cocked to either side, we are used to viewing the world in a certain way. As a result, most everything in a movie is balanced on a horizontal X-axis to mimic how we normally look at things around us. Not surprisingly, then, films that disrupt that equilibrium leave us unstable, struggling for normalcy. It's a great way to add suspense.

This technique is referred to as a canted angle (or Dutch angle) and involves turning the camera slightly to its side. The result is that we see images that aren't smoothly horizontal. Our mind tries to adjust to reassert what feels "right" to us. But the filmmaker wants us to understand that, for the characters, nothing feels right anymore.

Imbalance
in film noir

The Third Man
1949
Director: Carol Reed;
cinematography:
Robert Krasker;
actor: Joseph Cotten

1949's *The Third Man* illustrates how canted angles can insert tension and disorientation into a story. Director Carol Reed, working from Graham Greene's screenplay, introduces us to Holly (Joseph Cotten), an American novelist who lands in Vienna in search of his old pal Harry (Orson Welles), who wired him about a lucrative job opportunity. But when Holly arrives, he learns that Harry has died – although he quickly suspects that his friend's death was no accident.

This elegant black-and-white noir captures the paranoia and desperation of postwar Europe, but Reed's camerawork provides a vital extra component. Many of the film's shots incorporate canted angles, suggesting the intrigue and uncertainty that Holly faces while trying to get to the bottom of this mystery. The novelist doesn't know who he can trust, and the canted angles only ratchet up the intrigue as he weathers every twist and turn – including the shocking revelation that not only is Harry alive, but he's behind much of the wickedness Holly has uncovered in Vienna.

Reed and cinematographer Robert Krasker plunge us into a fraught, war-torn environment that's as much psychological as it is literal. Holly is stumbling through a bombed-out Vienna, but he's also trying to navigate the shocks he's absorbing about a friend he may never really have known at all. His inner and external worlds reflect one another. They're both out of balance.

A world that is out of whack

Sweeney Todd: The Demon Barber of Fleet Street
2007
Director: Tim Burton;
cinematography:
Dariusz Wolski;
actor: Johnny Depp

Tim Burton often uses canted angles, which is no surprise considering the worlds in which his movies are set. Whether in the comic-book universe of *Batman*, the sci-fi realm of *Mars Attacks!*, or the horror landscape of *Sleepy Hollow*, the veteran filmmaker loves surreal fantasy environments, where the rules of conventional society do not apply.

For his 2007 adaptation of *Sweeney Todd*, he cast frequent collaborator Johnny Depp to play the titular murderer who's out for revenge. The Stephen Sondheim musical is known for its dark humor and macabre themes, which makes this ideal terrain for Burton. The film's ominous production design (courtesy of art director Dante Ferretti and set decorator Francesca Lo Schiavo) won an Oscar, but it's also how Burton films his locales that gives them a sense of foreboding. The use of canted angles magnifies the unease that Todd's luckless victims experience as they confront this madman. In a sense, the warped perspective mirrors his deranged mind. In *Sweeney Todd*, it's almost as if we're living in his head.

The majesty

Gold Diggers of 1935
1935
Director: Busby Berkeley;
cinematography:
George Barnes

Filmmaker Wong Kar-wai is a master stylist, draping hyper-vivid films like *Chung-king Express* and *In the Mood for Love* in rich colors and swoony atmosphere. Another technique he incorporates is canted angles, which can be seen in his 1995 drama *Fallen Angels*. The film tells the story of several disaffected young people, but it's his camerawork that really instills in the viewer the sense of ennui that consumes his characters.

In an interview, Wong described his visual approach to *Fallen Angels*, saying he shot the film as if it was being documented by "civilian cameras ... they are always there watching people's behavior. In fact, they are the other main characters in the film." Wong's canted angles add to the intimacy and immediacy of the storytelling. Rather than being disorienting, the technique plunges us deeply into the emotional lives of his characters. We feel as deeply as the men and women of *Fallen Angels*, but we're also aware that these characters are being closely observed – by us. It's a style that calls attention to itself, but it helps communicate the themes Wong cares about.

Crane Shot

Placing the camera high above the action for a touch of grandeur and drama

Often, it makes sense to place your camera relatively close to the action. After all, that way the viewer can easily take in the most important elements of the scene. But certain moments call for a little extra grandeur, and that's when a crane shot might be preferable.

As shown in this behind-the-scenes photo from *Shakespeare in Love* (below), a crane shot involves placing a camera on a device that will lift it high above the actors. In modern filmmaking, the traditional crane shot can, in some instances, be simulated with a drone. But no matter how it's executed, crane shots give us a striking aerial view of a scene, allowing us to take in the enormity of a situation. And the only way to do that is to pull back.

Carnage

Gone with the Wind
1939
Director: Victor Fleming;
cinematography: Ernest
Haller; actor: Vivien Leigh

One of the most beloved American epics, *Gone with the Wind* is the tale of a grand, unrequited love affair between Scarlett O'Hara (Vivien Leigh) and Rhett Butler (Clark Gable). Its backdrop is just as grand, with the romantic drama taking place during the Civil War. During one stunning sequence, we get a sense of just how brutal that war was.

In the scene, Scarlett walks, as if in a daze, through a sea of wounded Confederate soldiers. As the crane shot pulls back and up, we begin to absorb the full horror of combat. Scarlett gets smaller in the frame, dwarfed by the sheer number of injured lying on the ground. We don't need to see her reaction. The sea of soldiers laid low by the war is the most important piece of information in the shot. Only by stepping back can we fully appreciate the moment's impact.

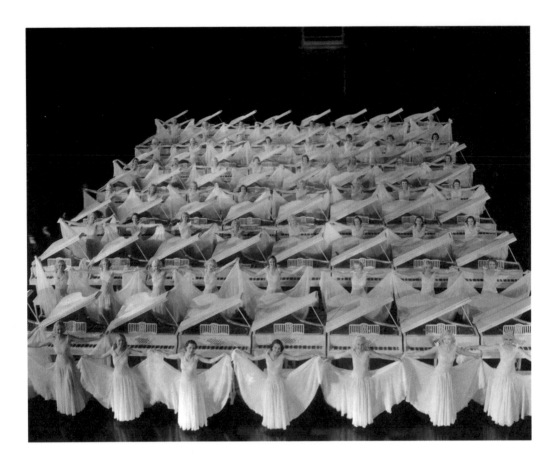

The majesty

Gold Diggers of 1935
1935
Director: Busby Berkeley;
cinematography:
George Barnes

Filmmaker Busby Berkeley once explained his unique approach to the movie musical: "I found out that the only way I could ever entertain the public was through that one eye of the camera. ... I felt I was unlimited – I felt that way at the time – so I would do different things that had never been done before, and they looked pretty good on the screen, and it led from one idea to another and one number to another and so on, and one picture to another."

One of those ideas was incorporating crane shots in his dance numbers. As we see here in *Gold Diggers of 1935*, that strategy creates a knockout effect. Sure, seeing just a couple of people dancing up close has power and intimacy. But Berkeley's approach gives us a majesty that's breathtaking. The massed choreography and uniformity is even more stunning. A crane shot amplifies the spectacle of the sequence.

The scale

Intolerance
1916
Director: D.W. Griffith;
cinematography:
Billy Bitzer

If you're going to chronicle the fall of a mighty empire, you need to first illustrate its mighty scale. That's what silent-era filmmaker D.W. Griffith achieves in *Intolerance*, which is, in part, about Babylon. For this sequence, he utilizes a crane shot that invites us to soak in the magnificence and electricity of an ancient metropolis.

But the crane shot has another effect. Hovering over the scene and drifting across it, Griffith's camera makes us feel as if we're being teleported back in time. We're allowed a privileged perspective, seeing an empire at its height before it's torn asunder. There's an appropriate grandeur to this *Intolerance* sequence; Griffith's floating camera makes the epochal moment feel appropriately epic.

Rule of Thirds

Splitting the frame into nine segments to highlight what's most visually interesting and important

When you're taking pictures of friends, the inclination may be to have that person right in the center of the frame. But if you try moving the camera to the left or right, putting your friend more on the side of the frame, it's an inherently more dynamic photo. There's an energy to the composition that it doesn't have when you just shoot your subject straight on.

What's known as the "rule of thirds" explains this principle. It's a concept that's existed since the eighteenth century, when it was applied to painting. But the idea is the same no matter the art form: When you divide a frame into nine symmetrical segments, the connecting points represent the most visually interesting places to locate your image's important elements. When you position your friend on the side of the frame while taking her photo, you're unconsciously obeying the rule of thirds. It's a concept filmmakers utilize all the time, even though we rarely notice.

Exposition in a more interesting way

Certified Copy
2010
Director: Abbas Kiarostami; cinematography: Luca Bigazzi; actor: Juliette Binoche

This still from the late Iranian filmmaker Abbas Kiarostami's *Certified Copy* is a very simple illustration of the rule of thirds. Juliette Binoche plays a gallery owner, and in this scene she's on the phone. Cellphone conversations are ubiquitous in our world, but they're not inherently cinematic. Kiarostami gets around this problem through framing. Binoche is angled toward the left of the screen, almost exactly on two intersecting points of our invisible grid. On the other two intersecting points is the empty countryside around her, which indicates how isolated she is.

Now, imagine if she was right in the middle of the frame. Binoche is a captivating actress, but there's only so much she could do with such a drab composition. Kiarostami adds a little drama and dynamism to the moment.

Playing with expectations

It's Complicated
2009
Director: Nancy Meyers;
cinematography: John Toll;
actor: Meryl Streep

Let's look at a promotional photo from *It's Complicated* to discuss how the rule of thirds can play with our assumptions about what's the most important element of an image. The film, written and directed by Nancy Meyers, is about Jane (Meryl Streep), a divorcée in a romantic triangle with two men, including her ex-husband. In this still, Jane is on the right side of the frame, her body lining up with two intersecting grid points. But in the center of the frame is a large plant that's nearly taller than she is.

Meyers is teasing our eye with this composition. We might be naturally drawn to the center of the screen, but we're confronted by an inanimate object that's clearly not the most important element of the scene. Then we notice Jane, almost like a surprise or an afterthought. It's a clever way to bring a little visual flair to a composition. (Also, the overall frame suggests that Jane is part of her environment, comfortable in her surroundings.)

By utilizing the rule of thirds, Meyers has created a more natural, lifelike composition – it's as if we've discovered Jane, rather than it being made obvious where to look.

Electricity between two characters

Shame
2011
Director: Steve McQueen;
cinematography:
Sean Bobbitt;
actors: Nicole Beharie,
Michael Fassbender

In *Shame*, Michael Fassbender plays Brandon, who is struggling with a sex addiction. Trying his hand at a more conventional relationship, he goes on a date with someone at his office, Marianne (Nicole Beharie). By this point in the movie, viewers know how powerful and debilitating his addiction is, and so we carry into the scene a certain amount of tension and suspense. How will this date go?

This image subtly suggests the electricity and wariness of their encounter. Director Steve McQueen positions his two actors exactly on the intersecting grid points, the most dynamic spots in the frame. If they were together in the center of the frame, it would seem that Brandon and Marianne are already very comfortable with one another. Instead, they're on those intersecting points, with a decent amount of empty space between them. Their smiles indicate a warmness between the characters, but the rule of thirds creates a dramatic undercurrent to an otherwise neutral moment. McQueen hints at a romantic spark that may or may not be growing.

Breaking the Fourth Wall

Erasing the barrier between audience and actor, bringing us into the action

You probably have heard the expression "breaking the fourth wall" and even know what it means. It's a narrative device in which a character speaks directly to the camera, as if she's addressing us directly. But while it may be self-explanatory, it's important to spend a quick moment explaining what that "fourth wall" is that's being broken.

The term finds its origins in theater. Typically, when you see a play, the action is framed by three walls: the one behind the actors and the two on the sides. The "fourth wall," in other words, is the one you don't see that separates the audience from the action. In most plays, that wall is never acknowledged, but it's a powerful yet fragile one. It's almost like a one-way mirror: We see through it to observe the characters, but they aren't aware of our presence.

Plays break the fourth wall all the time, but let's now focus on the technique in film. Loosely speaking, it occurs whenever a movie acknowledges that it's self-aware that it's a movie. For instance, in both versions of Michael Haneke's thriller *Funny Games*, a character uses a remote control to rewind the story so that a different outcome can occur. For our purposes, we're going to look at three instances in which the main character addresses the audience. But why they do is different.

The rebel

Ferris Bueller's Day Off
1986
Director: John Hughes;
cinematography:
Tak Fujimoto; actors:
Alan Ruck, Mia Sara,
Matthew Broderick

In this beloved teen comedy, Matthew Broderick plays Ferris Bueller, a smart-ass who ditches school along with his girlfriend (Mia Sara) and closest pal (Alan Ruck). Early in *Ferris Bueller's Day Off*, Ferris speaks directly to us. He explains to the audience how many sick days he's faked and what the best techniques are for fooling your parents into thinking you're not feeling well.

Writer–director John Hughes uses this narrative device to get us on the side of his rebellious character. Ferris seems to be confiding in us, taking us into his confidence, and we feel part of his inner circle because he's willing to share his innermost thoughts – which he doesn't with his own parents.

But this formal strategy also helps establish something essential about the character. In a "proper" film, the protagonist respects the fourth wall and maintains the illusion of the divide between viewer and character. But Ferris flouts the rules, hence his pride in playing hooky so he doesn't have to go to school. A mischievous protagonist like this won't adhere to narrative conventions. As soon as Ferris looks right into the camera, we know we're in the presence of someone who will do what he wants.

The friend

Amélie
2001
Director: Jean-Pierre
Jeunet; cinematography:
Bruno Delbonnel;
actor: Audrey Tautou

Audrey Tautou's Amélie is a peculiar protagonist. Blessed with a rich fantasy life and a resilient optimism, she decides that she wants to make the people around her happier by secretly working behind the scenes to give them what they've always wanted. Amélie could be an overly quirky character, but Tautou and director Jean-Pierre Jeunet work to ensure that we find her romantic spirit inspiring and endearing.

One of Jeunet's tricks is breaking the fourth wall. Amélie doesn't see the world like you and me, so it's only natural that she'd just start talking directly to the audience. In this way, *Amélie* invites us to see her as someone who wants to be our friend – as someone who wants to bring us into her world. A character who breaks the fourth wall can seem disruptive, violating the rules of drama. But in the case of *Amélie*, Jeunet strips away narrative strictures, bringing a greater warmth and intimacy to the storytelling. Amélie doesn't want us to be strangers, so she knocks the wall down that separates us from her.

The commentator

Deadpool
2016
Director: Tim Miller;
cinematography:
Ken Seng; actor:
Ryan Reynolds

Wade Wilson, the irreverent mercenary who will become Deadpool, doesn't seem like the sort of guy who becomes a superhero. He's too foul-mouthed, too self-centered, too cynical. No wonder, then, that in *Deadpool*, he doesn't behave like other comic-book characters. For one thing, he constantly talks to the camera, riffing on superhero conventions he has no intention of following.

Starring Ryan Reynolds, *Deadpool* loves threading pop-culture references through the narrative. It's a snotty, self-aware film that owns up to the fact that it's breaking the fourth wall in a similar way to *Ferris Bueller's Day Off*. (To make the connection more overt, the film ends the same way that the John Hughes comedy does, with Deadpool showing up after the credits to tell the audience to go home.)

Breaking the fourth wall is a clever way for a filmmaker to call attention to the clichés of a typical movie. A malcontent like Deadpool abhors the status quo. By addressing the audience, he's asking us to question all the artifice we normally see in our studio blockbusters.

Negative Space

Understanding that, sometimes, diminishing the characters in the frame can make for a powerful commentary

Our eye is naturally drawn to the most dynamic element of a scene. Usually, that's the main character, but sometimes the area around that individual is just as important – even if it seems like there's not much going on there. The concept of negative space might seem confusing – or counterintuitive – but as you'll see, the apparent emptiness around characters can be powerfully emotional or evocative. Even in the seeming nothingness, a lot can be occurring.

First, let's settle on a definition for negative space. It is, essentially, the background and surroundings around the central subject. Think of it this way: Negative space is the part of your passport or driver's license photo that *isn't* you. If you were taking a picture of friends or loved ones, you'd want to minimize the negative space, so that the people in the photo could be seen as clearly and as up-close as possible. And, ordinarily, that's the way directors will compose their shots, too. But let's examine three exceptions from movies of different eras and languages, exploring how each, in its own way, sharply harnesses what can be so affecting about negative space.

The impact of isolation and disconnection

L'Avventura
1960
Director: Michelangelo
Antonioni; cinematography:
Aldo Scavarda;
actors: Monica Vitti,
Gabriele Ferzetti

The first is *L'Avventura*, the acclaimed 1960 film from Italian director Michelangelo Antonioni. Widely derided at the time because of its unconventional approach, *L'Avventura* was soon embraced as a masterpiece, telling the story of a group of characters who are impacted by the disappearance of Anna (Lea Massari), a beautiful but enigmatic woman. However, Antonioni's film isn't a simple mystery-thriller; it is, instead, a rumination on disconnection and spiritual isolation.

These are themes that often feature in Antonioni's movies (*Red Desert*, *The Passenger*), and in *L'Avventura* he emphasizes his characters' existential despair by the way he films them. The director (working with cinematographer Aldo Scavarda) overwhelms the actors by making them relatively tiny in the frame, engulfed by their surroundings. The effect is twofold. First, we sense that this is unusual framing, and so there's a bit of disorientation on our part, mirroring the characters' inner anguish. Second, because the characters appear small, they give the impression of being weak and unexceptional. They have no power in the frame, just as they have no control over the uncertainty and sadness that consumes them. *L'Avventura* intentionally minimizes these people, never letting us forget how lost and feeble they feel in the modern world.

An intertwining of character and environment

Roma
2018
Director: Alfonso Cuarón;
cinematography: Alfonso
Cuarón; actors: Yalitza
Aparicio, Marco Graf

In other films, the location is as significant as the characters. Director Alfonso Cuarón's Oscar-winning *Roma* is a memory piece about the director's childhood in Mexico City in the early 1970s. Perhaps not surprisingly, then, the environment is a crucial component, which means that Cuarón often ensures that the background is in sharp focus so that we absorb the whole world around this fictional family and their loyal maid Cleo (Yalitza Aparicio).

As opposed to *L'Avventura*, though, note how *Roma* balances the actors and the negative space. We recognize that these characters reside in a busy, lively, sometimes chaotic city, but they're not overwhelmed by their surroundings. Rather, they are integrated into the visual landscape, not isolated or alienated. In Cuarón's mind, the characters and their setting are intertwined, which is a perceptive way of visualizing how memory works.

A dramatic moment in a casual setting

Punch-Drunk Love
2002
Director: Paul
Thomas Anderson;
cinematography: Robert
Elswit; actors: Emily
Watson, Adam Sandler

Lastly, let's look at *Punch-Drunk Love*, which tells the unlikely love story between an anxious man, Barry (Adam Sandler), and his patient, hesitant new girlfriend Lena (Emily Watson). Writer–director Paul Thomas Anderson incorporates several unusual techniques for this offbeat romantic comedy – including lens flare and a discordant sound design – to suggest how strange, even alien, attraction can be. But because Barry also seems to have emotional problems, Anderson dramatizes his character's struggle through negative space, placing him in the distance or the corner of the frame.

However, during one of the film's most romantic moments, *Punch-Drunk Love* illustrates another use of negative space. Near the movie's end, Barry reunites with his beloved in Hawaii. But instead of putting the characters' kiss front and center, Anderson pulls the camera back so that we see them in silhouette, the surroundings dominating the frame. Here, negative space creates a casualness for this critical scene. We feel like we're spying on something – almost as if we were observing this whole tableau and just happened to notice the couple's embrace. The negative space makes the scene more dynamic, more special, than if it was shot conventionally.

Normally, your protagonists are the most important element. But that doesn't mean they need to dominate the frame. Give a thought to how negative space can complement (or comment on) what we're watching.

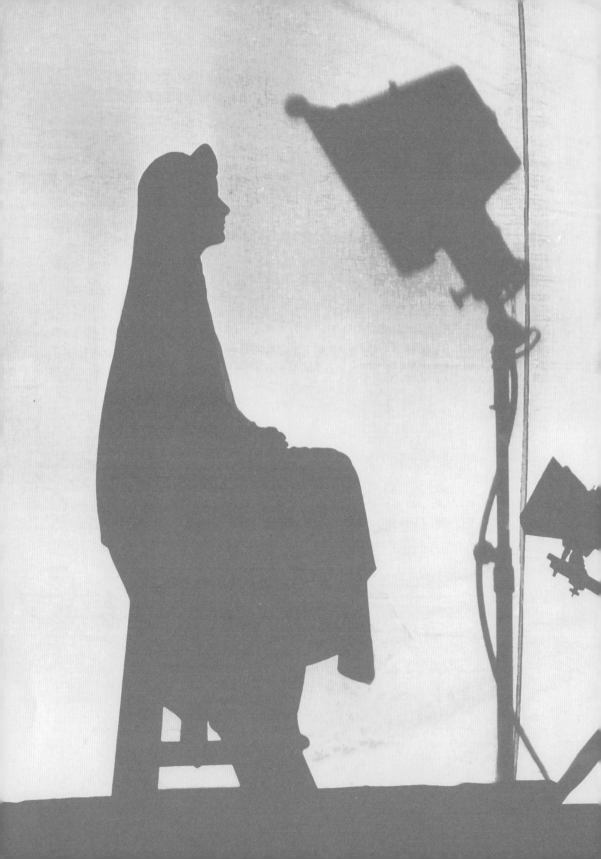

LIGHTING & CAMERA

Deep Focus

Filling the frame with images we need to see

In most movies, the director and cinematographer choose what captures our eye through a simple technique: They put the scene's most important element into focus. It's an easy way to let a viewer know what to watch on-screen, but it contradicts how human beings actually experience real life, where everything on the same plane is equally visible.

By comparison, deep focus photography allows the entire frame to be seen sharply, whether it's in the foreground or background. On a technical level, the effect is achieved by incorporating a wide-angle lens – with a short focal length and a small aperture – and placing the camera further away from the action. However, this will also require the filmmaker to ensure that everything in the frame is placed exactly how he or she wants it, since the viewer will be able to read all the information in the frame.

As a result, it's not always obvious what is the most important element in the scene, thereby forcing the viewer to take in the whole image. But rather than confusing audiences, deep focus offers a new level of drama and immersion into a story.

Drama

Citizen Kane
1941
Cinematography:
Gregg Toland; director:
Orson Welles; actors:
Dorothy Comingore,
Orson Welles, Ruth
Warrick, Ray Collins

Orson Welles's most acclaimed movie is a dazzling demonstration of deep focus. Working with cinematographer Gregg Toland, Welles chose the technique to achieve a sense of realism. But it also emulated the feel of live theater, where Welles had made his name before turning to filmmaking. Onstage, everything is visible to the audience, and likewise *Citizen Kane*'s frames are alive with people moving through their environment.

One such example is the dramatic moment in which Charles Foster Kane's affair with the singer Susan Alexander (Dorothy Comingore) is about to be exposed (Kane's political rival, Jim Gettys, will alert the media, as well as Kane's wife Emily). In this frame, we see all four characters, their grim expressions all in focus. In addition, the background can be seen clearly. Deep focus gives the scene electricity – Kane's whole world is collapsing, and we can't look away.

Horror

The Innocents
1961
Cinematography:
Freddie Francis;
director: Jack Clayton;
actor: Deborah Kerr

In horror movies, what we can't see – something hidden in the shadows, for instance – can be terrifying. The unknown is a powerful tool for directors. But for *The Innocents*, director Jack Clayton and cinematographer Freddie Francis incorporated deep focus photography, which would seem to be counterintuitive. If we can see everything in the frame, then what could scare us?

The film concerns Miss Giddens (Deborah Kerr), the governess of two young children, Flora (Pamela Franklin) and Miles (Martin Stephens), who live in a mansion that may be haunted. By putting every inch of the house in focus, our eye is anxiously drawn to different elements in the frame. Where could the evil be coming from? The effect is disconcerting and claustrophobic. *The Innocents* is a superb example of atmospheric psychological horror – because deep focus isn't usually implemented in movies, the technique only enhances the uneasy feeling we have watching this spooky film.

Comedy

The Rules of the Game
1939
Cinematography:
Jean Bachelet;
director: Jean Renoir;
actors: Julien Carette,
Gaston Modot

Welles and *Citizen Kane* didn't invent deep focus. French filmmaker Jean Renoir brilliantly utilized the photographic style for his 1939 masterpiece, a cutting satire about a group of wealthy individuals spending some time at a country estate. Renoir and cinematographer Jean Bachelet wanted the viewer to pay attention to every character – even if they were in the background seemingly doing nothing – in order to suggest how alike all these amoral individuals were. In order to do that, deep focus was essential.

But beyond creating a sense of thematic linking between different characters, *The Rules of the Game*'s deep focus stripped away the artificiality of film. Renoir's lens was more like our own eye, creating a lifelike feel to the movie's comedy and tragedy. This was not a light escapist farce – quite the opposite: Renoir wanted to hold a mirror up to his society, whether viewers wanted to see it or not. "People go to the cinema in the hope of forgetting their everyday problems," the director once said, "and it was precisely their own worries that I plunged them into." In truth, he was asking them to focus on the social ills all around them.

Chiaroscuro

Articulating mood and suspense through shadows and light

Often, filmmakers will alert us to what's most important on screen by putting the protagonist in focus and leaving everything in the background fuzzy. But that's not the only way to highlight a crucial character. By incorporating chiaroscuro lighting, a director draws our attention in a far moodier way. The main character will be brightly lit while his surroundings are shrouded in darkness.

The effect goes back to painting, where artists such as Caravaggio and Rembrandt developed the notion that their subjects would look far more dynamic with high-contrast lighting. Modern cinematographers utilize a similar technique, playing with dark and light in the same frame. In a sense, darkness gives light more power. And that contrast causes tension.

A world of darkness

The Godfather
1972
Cinematography:
Gordon Willis; director:
Francis Ford Coppola;
actors: Salvatore Corsitto,
Marlon Brando

The Godfather was shot by Gordon Willis, a master cinematographer nicknamed "the Prince of Darkness" for his stellar use of chiaroscuro lighting. Just about any still from any of the three movies in that Francis Ford Coppola trilogy would be instructive, but we'll use this one for our purposes.

The scene takes place in the offices of Don Corleone (Marlon Brando), a mafia boss who uses his power sparingly but efficiently. He sees himself as just another businessman, but *The Godfather* constantly reminds us that Corleone's world is a brutal distortion of the American dream. Crime and murder are omnipresent, as is evil.

This image captures that dichotomy brilliantly. Corleone is brightly lit, but the background is pitch black. Sunlight coming through the window may illuminate the space somewhat – as does a wall light in the corner – but there remains a piercing blackness throughout the scene. And what is that blackness? Metaphorically, it's the wickedness that consumes these characters, who must often kill to maintain their power. It's a beautifully shot scene, but also a richly evocative one.

In a noir mood

Touch of Evil
1958
Cinematography:
Russell Metty;
director: Orson Welles;
actor: Orson Welles

Film noir made great use of chiaroscuro lighting. Directors understood that the high-contrast lighting, paired with black-and-white imagery, could create environments in which suspicion and malevolence were everywhere – a perfect cinematic cocktail for mysteries and thrillers.

One of the finest film noirs is *Touch of Evil*, which found director Orson Welles and cinematographer Russell Metty plunging us into a landscape of murder and paranoia. Charlton Heston's Mexican lawman is the one source of virtue in a film dominated by corruption, personified by Welles's crooked cop Quinlan.

In this image, we see how shadows cover one side of Quinlan's face. In a more traditional film, the cinematographer would add a little fill light so we could see all of Welles illuminated. But those shadows suggest the moral rot within the character, and the world in which he lives.

A waking nightmare

The Night of the Hunter
1955
Cinematography:
Stanley Cortez;
director: Charles
Laughton; actors:
Shelley Winters,
Robert Mitchum

In *The Night of the Hunter*, Robert Mitchum plays Harry Powell, a seemingly upstanding preacher who carries a dark secret: He's really a murderer. The film concerns Powell's insidious attempt to find some money left behind by a dead comrade, insinuating himself into the deceased man's family.

That's a devious plan, and *The Night of the Hunter* communicates the gathering evil by using chiaroscuro lighting. This still image is an apt illustration. Mitchum's face is illuminated, but his neck is plunged into darkness, and the room around him is an uneasy mix of light and shadow.

There's a nightmarish quality to the way that director Charles Laughton and cinematographer Stanley Cortez film these scenes, drawing from the high-contrast style of German Expressionism (*The Cabinet of Dr. Caligari*), which helped popularize chiaroscuro lighting. This family doesn't realize it, but Powell's no man of God. As the tense lighting suggests, he's closer to the devil.

Key Light and Fill Light

Illuminating your actors so that their reactions are clearly visible, while also offering shading and definition

The most traditional way to light an actor is to use what's commonly known as three-point lighting. This consists of the key light, fill light and back light. Here, we'll primarily focus on the first two components, which provide the primary lighting source (key light) and then a secondary source (fill light) that adds a little dimensionality to the subject. (Back light is a source of light behind the actor that's aimed toward the camera.)

Not every shot needs three-point lighting, or even fill light. The situation will dictate what sort of lighting setup you'll want. But let's examine a few films to see how different setups can create a precise, memorable look.

The traditional look

Mudbound
2017
Cinematography:
Rachel Morrison;
director: Dee Rees;
actor: Carey Mulligan

In *Mudbound*, a white family and a Black family reluctantly must work together to keep a Mississippi farm afloat during the late 1930s. Carey Mulligan plays Laura, the long-suffering wife of the unkind Henry (Jason Clarke), and in this shot we clearly see her anguish. Directed by Dee Rees and shot by Rachel Morrison, *Mudbound* aims for a realistic depiction of life among the working poor, and as a result the lighting is equally naturalistic.

In this image, the key light is shining on Mulligan from the left (we can tell because, from our perspective, the left side of her face is more brightly illuminated, although technically it's *her* right side). But a little fill light is used so that we can also see the other side of her face. At the same time, back light allows her to stand out a bit from the background.

This is a classically lit shot without calling too much attention to itself. The lighting design is all working in concert so that it looks like sunlight and other natural light sources. It's one of the most important tasks for any director of photography: composing a lighting scheme that perfectly mimics real life.

A sharp contrast

Daughters of the Dust
1991
Cinematography: Arthur Jafa; director: Julie Dash; actors: Althea Lang, Geraldine Dunston, Cheryl Lynn Bruce, Adisa Anderson, Cora Lee Day, Kaycee Moore

Daughters of the Dust has the feel of myth, as writer–director Julie Dash chronicles a family's difficult decision at the dawn of the 1900s: Should they stay isolated on their idyllic island off the east coast of the United States, or should they go to the mainland and integrate into society? This sunny paradise provides excellent lighting opportunities for Dash and cinematographer Arthur Jafa.

The first still illustrates what your subject can look like with intense key light but no fill light. The sun hits the side of her face, casting the other side into shadow. It creates a striking composition, and it makes sense for the environment where Dash is shooting. (In the real situation, there wouldn't be some magical fill light illuminating the other side of her face.)

"We shot in all natural light," Dash told me in 2016. "[Jafa] created various handmade reflectors to balance and bounce light and to fill in [in order] to adjust and compensate for those black skins against white sand, which is very, very difficult." Indeed, in *Daughters of the Dust*, the actors' faces are superbly lit, not nearly as contrasty as in this first promotional still. Consider the second image, which is more in keeping with the final film. By using reflectors, you can create seamless fill light in natural settings.

A little pizzazz

*We Need to Talk
About Kevin*
2011
Cinematography:
Seamus McGarvey;
director: Lynne Ramsay;
actor: Tilda Swinton

Mood lighting can help inform how we feel about a character – or help communicate her state of mind. Take *We Need to Talk About Kevin*, about a grieving mother, Eva (Tilda Swinton), grappling with a tragic past. Director Lynne Ramsay and cinematographer Seamus McGarvey show Eva in her isolation and sorrow, occasionally making innovative use of key light and fill light to craft a psychological snapshot of this woman.

In this shot, she's at a diner at Christmastime. Red light comes pouring in through the window on the right side of the frame. The overhead fluorescent lights provide illumination from the other side. Consequently, Eva's face is split nearly in half between the two light sources.

It's a beautiful way to suggest the mental fracturing going on within Eva. Guilt, shame and sadness consume her – she's a pariah in her community because of a horrific act her son committed. This shot invisibly suggests all that trauma and anguish, simply by the filmmakers' choice of how to use key light and fill light. This novel lighting scheme helps us see the character – but also to truly see where she is emotionally.

Low Light

Shooting in darkened locations without losing the drama

Earlier, we discussed chiaroscuro lighting, which is a very specific style of shooting. Here, we will look more broadly at scenes that, because of setting or filmmaker preference, require extremely low light. Obviously, they will require the cinematographer to widen the aperture in order to let enough light in, but cutting-edge digital cameras have made low-light shooting far less onerous than in generations past.

Even then, though, the fear is that audiences will have a tough time making out the information you want to convey on the screen. Wouldn't it just be easier to let a little more light in? We'll take a close look at three examples of darkness giving scenes an extra resonance.

The otherworldly

*The Assassination of
Jesse James by the
Coward Robert Ford*
2007
Cinematography: Roger
Deakins; director: Andrew
Dominik; actor: Brad Pitt

Chronicling the final year in the life of the bandit Jesse James (Brad Pitt), film-maker Andrew Dominik seeks to marry realism and folklore, presenting us with an epic that's both grounded and ethereal – almost as if we're thumbing through the pages of a dusty old history book flecked with magic. That may sound like an overly precious way to describe *The Assassination of Jesse James*, but the director (teamed with cinematographer Roger Deakins) gives us a movie with an otherworldly glow, especially in its nighttime shots.

This still indicates how low light works in *The Assassination of Jesse James*. We can't make out much of James, but we don't need to. As he's photographed here, he's larger than life – a legend who walks among us. Note how his silhou-etted body conveys menace and strength, while the oncoming train adds energy and tension to the scene – we sense that these two forces will soon collide. And, of course, a daring heist like this would work best at night, so it's under-standable why James would pick this moment to rob the train. It's a beautiful image, no extra lighting required.

The stylish

Solo: A Star Wars Story
2018
Cinematography:
Bradford Young;
director: Ron Howard;
actor: Donald Glover

Bradford Young is one of our best young cinematographers, earning accolades for shooting everything from the sci-fi drama *Arrival* to the period piece *Selma*. His work on *Solo* is especially daring because, like many of his films, it's much darker than the typical studio effort. And we don't mean "darker" in terms of tone – we're talking about the amount of light he uses in his compositions. At first, it might be jarring to see a *Star Wars* film this murky. But soon, it becomes apparent how effective his lighting strategy is.

In the movie, Donald Glover plays a young Lando Calrissian. At first blush, this image might look like it's been poorly lit. But Young's photography adds layers of texture and intrigue to the *Star Wars* legend. Of course, it's also incredibly stylish, hinting at the moral ambiguity of film noir. As a result, *Solo* has far more mood and grittiness than other chapters of the George Lucas space saga.

Back in 2018, Young acknowledged that he prefers a darker visual palette than other cinematographers. "I am well aware of how dark my work has become," he said at the time, "but it's a response to the atmosphere, politically, socially and culturally. That darkness, for me, is not just technical. It's psychological, from a dark place – it's taken me a long time to say that." His stunning images speak for themselves.

The realistic

Zero Dark Thirty
2012
Cinematography:
Greig Fraser; director:
Kathryn Bigelow

Zero Dark Thirty depicts the dogged pursuit of Osama bin Laden after the 9/11 attacks. Director Kathryn Bigelow opted for a matter-of-fact chronicling of this years-long manhunt, jettisoning Hollywood blockbuster theatrics for plenty of stripped-down drama. But at the film's end, we watch intently as Navy SEALs storm bin Laden's compound and kill him. Even then, though, *Zero Dark Thirty* refuses to be a traditional action film, and you can tell this because so much of the photography is incredibly dark.

The above still is instructional because it's actually been lightened – the actual sequence is far murkier than this. Because the raid was executed in the dead of night, Bigelow chooses to be as realistic as she can in the sequence. As a result, part of the suspense is that, even with night-vision goggles, it can be difficult to see – both for the characters and for us.

But amid that realism, there was also style. "The idea was that it was supposed to be very impressionistic," said cinematographer Greig Fraser, "it was supposed to not make you feel like you're watching a Hollywood rendition of a Navy SEAL raid. … You're basically recreating what's happening with the stars. With stars at night there is no ambience, but there is light, stars put out light, but very little." That's why we don't mind that we can't make out every inch of the frame – the low-light look feels accurate to what the situation would be like in real life.

Golden Hour

Capturing the ethereal glow of a setting (or rising) sun to create a little movie magic

It's often beautiful when the sun is rising or setting, the light adorning the sky in a way unlike at any other time of day. This brief window is referred to as golden hour, and it can be a potent tool for filmmakers.

There's something ineffably beautiful about golden hour – the light has an almost dreamlike quality to it. Painters used sunrises and sunsets to give their landscape portraits a heavenly glow, and directors have borrowed the technique to suggest emotions without having their characters say a word.

Fragility

To the Wonder
2012
Cinematography:
Emmanuel Lubezki;
director: Terrence Malick;
actor: Rachel McAdams

Perhaps the king of golden hour photography is Terrence Malick. Starting with 1973's *Badlands*, the writer–director has often studied how human beings clash or commune with the natural world, and he's a filmmaker who's as invested in a blade of grass as the emotional tumult within his characters. 1978's *Days of Heaven* was filmed primarily during golden hour, and ever since he's relied on natural light to give his movies an ethereal tone.

For our purposes, let's consider *To the Wonder*, his 2012 study of restless souls all trying (and failing) to find romantic contentment. This still depicts Jane (Rachel McAdams), a rancher hung up on Ben Affleck's Neil. We sense her spiritual disillusionment because of her resigned pose and the wide-open space around her. But the light is also crucial. It almost appears as if she's caught in a purgatory. Just from looking at the photo, it's not clear if the sun is sinking or rising, and likewise Jane is uncertain, stuck in a moment.

Golden hour lighting is gorgeous, but it can also be melancholic, hinting at the dying of the light or the fragility of a new day. *To the Wonder* evokes so many emotions from such a simple lighting choice.

Time running short

Before Sunset
2004
Cinematography:
Lee Daniel; director:
Richard Linklater; actors:
Ethan Hawke, Julie Delpy

Before Sunset was the follow-up film to *Before Sunrise*, reuniting one-time lovers Jesse (Ethan Hawke) and Céline (Julie Delpy) in Paris as they catch up on each other's lives. But as the sun starts to set and Jesse has to catch a plane, they realize that their reminiscence is running short – they will have to decide whether to rekindle that spark or let it fizzle.

Director Richard Linklater uses his story's time frame to his advantage, incorporating golden hour photography to amplify the romance, as well as the ephemeral nature of true love. Both Jesse and Céline realize how fleeting their time together is – the honeyed light only makes that fact more poignant.

This still is suffused with sadness, underlining how short this moment of reconnection is. Soon, the light will go out. Will their second chance fade away as well?

Evoking
the past

War Horse
2011
Cinematography:
Janusz Kamiński; director:
Steven Spielberg

Steven Spielberg's *War Horse* is a period piece that takes place in the early twentieth century, in the shadow of World War I. Consciously made in a way that evokes older movies, this drama makes good use of golden hour lighting to conjure up the past.

Let's examine this promotional still to get a sense of how Spielberg and cinematographer Janusz Kamiński achieved their effects. What's most striking initially is the power of the sun, which is like a fireball slowly descending in the sky. As a result, the light is evocative and nostalgic, calling to mind all the drama and mournfulness of war. There's a funereal quality to the lighting, but also a grandeur. These silhouetted soldiers seem to be enshrined for posterity in this shot – weary men on horseback trudging across the landscape in between bloody battles.

This *War Horse* scene is stirring, and much of its strength comes from the time of day when it was shot. Golden hour can be surprisingly emotional.

Slow Motion

Decelerating the action, intensifying the emotions

Most cinematic images are shot 24 frames per second, which mimics how the human eye takes in information. If you increase that frame rate when filming, but play it back at 24 frames per second, something interesting happens: The images seem slowed down. In the early days of film, this technique required the camera operator to overcrank in order to shoot more frames per second. With modern technology, your frame rate can be switched with the push of a button.

Whether then or now, however, the question remains the same: Why are you utilizing slow motion? It's a popular cinematic device with obvious benefits, but a filmmaker needs to be careful not to overuse it. Still, when wielded properly, slow motion is a dazzling narrative weapon.

Exuding cool

Reservoir Dogs
1992
Cinematography:
Andrzej Sekuła; director:
Quentin Tarantino; actors:
Michael Madsen, Quentin
Tarantino, Harvey Keitel,
Chris Penn, Lawrence
Tierney, Tim Roth, Steve
Buscemi, Eddie Bunker

Writer–director Quentin Tarantino launched onto the scene with this 1992 thriller about a group of criminals working together to pull off a heist. Given nicknames such as Mr. Pink and Mr. Brown, and wearing the same nondescript suit-and-tie ensemble, the thieves had a striking anonymity from the film's earliest moments. To further emphasize his characters' iconic cool, Tarantino had them walk in slow motion during the opening credits.

Reservoir Dogs has plenty of scenes that were widely parodied and referenced in future films, but the slow-mo introduction is among the movie's most famous. In Tarantino's hands, the device elevates these wisecracking, two-bit hoods into far more compelling figures. Slow motion bestows on them a sense of gravitas and grandeur, making their every movement seem meaningful. Earlier in the film, they were joking about menial things, like the ethics of not tipping a waitress. But in this sequence, they're imbued with cinematic import.

(Quick note: Because *Reservoir Dogs* became such an influential film of the 1990s, other directors used slow motion to mock their own characters' attempts at coolness. Most memorably, the horny, clueless young men of *Swingers* discuss *Reservoir Dogs* before going out on the town. Director Doug Liman intentionally mimicked the Tarantino slow-mo shot, illustrating how much less dangerous his characters were than Tarantino's.)

Memorializing tragedy

Bonnie and Clyde
1967
Cinematography:
Burnett Guffey;
director: Arthur Penn;
actor: Faye Dunaway

The groundbreaking *Bonnie and Clyde* rewrote the rules of Hollywood studio films, ushering in a new era of risk-taking and a focus on movies about youth culture. Director Arthur Penn also introduced a new frankness around violence, ending the crime drama with the traumatic deaths of Bonnie Parker (Faye Dunaway) and Clyde Barrow (Warren Beatty) in a hail of bullets. It wasn't just that we saw our main characters die in such brutal, pitiless fashion – it's that we saw it in slow motion.

This infamous scene illustrates the technique's power. For one thing, slow-mo makes every twitch of their pained bodies seem more agonizing. We feel the violence on a visceral level because Penn lingers on the human carnage. In addition, slow motion underlines how dramatic this moment is. If Bonnie and Clyde died in real time, it would be fast and quick. With slow motion, their bloody demise feels significant, a tragedy. Penn memorializes the last few seconds of their lives, letting the impact of their deaths fully sink in.

Adding excitement

The Matrix
1999
Cinematography: Bill
Pope; directors: Lana
and Lilly Wachowski;
actor: Keanu Reeves

Lana and Lilly Wachowski blew minds with their 1999 masterwork, including how they incorporated slow motion into action scenes. Their most famous innovation was the use of what's known as "bullet time" technology, a special effect that involves the camera circling around the actors. When audiences see the scene in the theater, it appears that we're observing this movement in slow motion.

The Matrix gives us a world in which the impossible is possible, and so slow motion is a useful narrative tool. A key component to the story is that average guy Neo (Keanu Reeves) comes to understand that he's the chosen one who can save humanity from the tyranny of evil machines. As part of his hero's journey, Neo will learn to harness untapped powers within himself, including the ability to move at lightning speed. To dramatize his raised awareness, the filmmakers chose slow motion, which made it look like Neo was swift enough to avoid bullets. By changing our perception of reality and distorting time itself, the Wachowskis added extra excitement to a stunning blockbuster.

Panning

Moving the camera from a fixed point in order to take in all the action

When we stand still but turn our head from side to side to take in something, we're replicating what goes on in a panning shot. It's a pretty simple move: The operator has the camera on a tripod or other fixed position, and then he rotates the camera from right to left, or left to right.

We're so used to camera movements that are a little more dynamic that a pan might not seem that exciting. But that can be part of its sneaky appeal. Many panning shots are deceptively serene, almost as if the camera is slowly surveying the environment to take in all the surroundings. But that only sets us up for a surprise – or helps establish a particular tone that the filmmaker is seeking.

Setting a world

The Last Picture Show
1971
Cinematography:
Robert Surtees; director:
Peter Bogdanovich

Peter Bogdanovich's bittersweet portrait of a dying small town introduces its central theme immediately. The opening shot pans across the main street of Anarene, a desolate Texas town, and we hear driving wind on the soundtrack. If you didn't know better, you'd swear everyone has cleared out, leaving just a few empty buildings to gather dust and tumbleweeds.

The slow pan accomplishes a few things. First, it's a way for *The Last Picture Show* to welcome us into its world, inviting the viewer to literally take a look around Anarene. As much as we'll get to know the film's main characters, the setting is almost as important, and so this shot asks us to consider the community as a whole.

Additionally, the panning shot sets a tone. Taking place in the early 1950s, *The Last Picture Show* is a movie about what happens when people and places are left behind, so it's not surprising that the film has a melancholic air. The deliberate pace of the camera move suggests that we're in a town (and also a film) that's a little sleepy. This isn't a place where action-packed excitement occurs. Bogdanovich's panning shot slows down our rhythms, preparing us for the quiet, thoughtful story to come.

Mimicking
our eyes

The Lobster
2015
Cinematography: Thimios
Bakatakis; director:
Yorgos Lanthimos; actor:
Jacqueline Abrahams

Just because a panning shot occurs from a fixed point, that doesn't mean the fixed point has to be stationary. The opening of *The Lobster* cleverly illustrates how a pan can catch us off guard. The movie is about a near-future in which all human adults must be paired off with a mate. If they're not, they're turned into an animal. We'll meet *The Lobster*'s central characters soon enough, but the opening puts us in the mood for the surreal dark comedy that will follow.

As the film begins, a character we'll never see again (Jacqueline Abrahams) drives dispassionately through the countryside. All in one unbroken shot, she pulls her car to the side of the road and gets out. The camera, positioned just outside the vehicle, suddenly pans left to follow her as she approaches some donkeys in a field. What happens next is shocking: She shoots one of them dead with chilly precision and intent. Her mission accomplished, she walks back to the car.

Director Yorgos Lanthimos, known for twisted satires such as *Dogtooth* and *The Favourite*, utilizes the smoothness of a panning shot to show us something horrifying. But the camera is also mimicking how we view the world. Lanthimos's lens is, essentially, turning its head to the left to see what the character is doing, just as we'd be inclined to do in that moment. But we can't possibly anticipate what our "eyes" are about to see.

PM 10:13:53

Creating fear

Paranormal Activity 3
2011
Cinematography:
Magdalena Górka;
directors: Henry Joost
and Ariel Schulman;
actor: Johanna Braddy

One of the most ingenious uses of a panning shot can be found in *Paranormal Activity 3*, which brings fresh ideas to the popular found-footage horror franchise by introducing a novel new place to stick a camera.

In the previous installments, audiences had become accustomed to the films' conceit, "seeing" the movie from the perspective of security cameras, camcorders and other recording devices deployed by the main characters. But for *Paranormal Activity 3*, directors Henry Joost and Ariel Schulman have their homeowners (Chris Smith and Lauren Bittner) strap a camera to an oscillating fan downstairs so that it can record everything that happens in two rooms. For once, we don't have a static shot of terrifying occurrences. Here, the camera *moves*, hinting at horrible sights and then coyly panning away, only to pan back and pay off the suspense.

Speaking to *Entertainment Weekly* in 2011, Joost said, "It turns out to be the perfect horror movie camera technique. No one's controlling the camera, so every time it pans away, you're like 'No!' You know something's going to happen when it's panning away. ... If you film it right, you can get the audience to physically adjust in their seats, and we knew we wanted to make an interactive movie, so we thought, 'Can we come up with a camera technique that will get people to try to see beyond the frame?'" Indeed, no panning shot in cinema might be scarier than this one.

Steadicam

Utilizing a crucial piece of camera technology to simulate the feeling of agile, controlled motion

Invented in 1975 by Garrett Brown, the Steadicam revolutionized camerawork, giving cinematographers and directors a device that could create a smooth movement through a space. Sturdier than handheld shots, Steadicam gives the impression that the camera is floating, an effect that can be ghostly, ethereal, transporting or unnerving. People commonly think of a Steadicam as a camera but, in fact, it's the mount that's attached to the camera, allowing the operator to navigate through a location without worrying about shaking the camera.

But, as Brown himself acknowledged, his invention is simply a tool like any other. "By itself, it doesn't do a thing," he told *No Film School* in 2016. "In the hands of a gifted operator, it is an instrument and is of no more use than the skill of the operator. It just barely allows a gifted human being to do this amazing trick: to run along with their ever-moving corpus. Out the other end comes an astonishing dolly shot smooth as glass." Gifted filmmakers have been making good use of his invention for more than 40 years.

The dread

The Shining
1980
Cinematography:
John Alcott; director:
Stanley Kubrick; actor:
Jack Nicholson

Director Stanley Kubrick utilized Steadicam for his terrifying adaptation of the Stephen King novel. Indeed, *The Shining* is probably the most famous example of what Brown's creation can do. In telling the story of Jack (Jack Nicholson), a failed writer who goes mad while caretaking the Overlook Hotel, Kubrick thought of several ways to leave his audience ill at ease. What the Steadicam allowed was a palpable sense of dread in every camera movement. The smoothness of the shots felt inhuman, chilly – a perfect mindset in which to place the audience when you're making a horror film.

The ethereal

The Tree of Life
2011
Cinematography:
Emmanuel Lubezki;
director: Terrence
Malick; actors: Jessica
Chastain, Tye Sheridan

In his twenty-first-century work, writer–director Terrence Malick has shifted primarily to Steadicam shots. To understand his rationale, look no further than *The Tree of Life*, which follows a Texas family headed by a stoic father (Brad Pitt) and a loving mother (Jessica Chastain). Malick drew from childhood recollections to craft the narrative, and the movie contains an undeniable autobiographical streak. But among its unique components is its camerawork.

Much of *The Tree of Life* wrestles with the very nature of existence, and our relationship with the cosmic. Faith is a crucial component of the film, as the characters offer silent prayers (through voiceover) to God. Steadicam enhances Malick's narrative goals in two ways. First, the seemingly floating camera gives these realistic scenes a surrealistic quality, inviting us to notice how extraordinary everyday moments are. Second, Steadicam can create an otherworldly perspective, almost as if we're floating above the story. In other words, it's a Godlike vantage point, and so we feel the presence of a heavenly figure observing this family as they experience tragedy, regret and fleeting moments of happiness.

There was another advantage to this shooting style. Malick wanted *The Tree of Life* to feel spontaneous, and so he incorporated Steadicam and handheld cameras, shooting on the fly to capture the actors as they experimented with the scenes. This improvisation can be felt in the final film: Those hovering shots feel like they're witness to unrehearsed, magical moments.

The magic trick

Birdman
2014
Cinematography:
Emmanuel Lubezki;
director: Alejandro
González Iñárritu;
actor: Michael Keaton

The Oscar-winning *Birdman* satirizes the artistic aspirations of washed-up movie star Riggan Thomson (Michael Keaton), following him on a madcap day in what looks like one continuous scene. That was done through digital trickery, of course, partly thanks to the smooth movements of a Steadicam.

"We mapped everything out, which allowed us to time the dialogue through the corridors and other scenes," Steadicam operator Chris Haarhoff said in a 2014 interview. "All the doors were marked and all the pertinent moments and geographical aspects were noted so we could rehearse."

Because Steadicam provides a slight unreality, *Birdman*'s comedy and drama – not to mention the film's portrait of the ego and insecurity of actors – has a warped, hall-of-mirrors strangeness to it. We glide through the space alongside Riggan as he tries to balance family and career, the high-wire camera movements always in danger of collapsing into chaos. Steadicam holds *Birdman*'s tension while helping to sell the movie's impressive technical prowess.

Handheld

Taking the camera off the sticks
and embracing the unsteadiness
of real life

We're used to most shots in cinema being smooth – even if they have motion, they glide rather than shake. But sometimes, a director will incorporate camerawork that isn't so steady in order to elicit particular emotional responses.

Not all handheld shots are wild. Plenty of documentarians take the camera off the tripod (or sticks) when capturing images in an unpredictable environment (indeed, the whole school of *cinéma vérité* nonfiction filmmaking emphasizes embedding oneself with your subjects in order to create the most realistic depiction of their world, often utilizing handheld cameras). But narrative storytellers have borrowed the technique from documentary filmmakers to give their movies a sense of gritty realism. As a result, viewers have come to associate the irregular movements of handheld cameras with the volatility of everyday life.

When a director chooses to go handheld, it's not by accident, even if the camerawork seems to look more haphazard.

Spontaneity

Husbands and Wives
1992
Cinematography:
Carlo Di Palma; director:
Woody Allen; actors:
Liam Neeson, Mia Farrow

When Woody Allen prepared to shoot *Husbands and Wives*, about two imperiled marriages, he decided to set aside the polished, stately camerawork that's one of the hallmarks of his oeuvre. As he once explained, "I've always been thinking that so much time is wasted and so much is devoted to the prettiness of films and the delicacy and the precision. And I said to myself, why not just start to make some films where only the content is important. Pick up the camera, forget about the dolly, just hand-hold the thing and get what you can."

The result was one of Allen's rawest films. The writer–director taps into the anger and disillusionment that occurs when love sours, and the livewire performances are enhanced by the handheld camerawork, which seems to be eavesdropping on these characters at their most intimate and vulnerable moments. *Husbands and Wives* features breakups and flirtations, endings and beginnings, and there's a spontaneity to the acting that, arguably, was a rewarding by-product of the looser filming environment.

Of course, using handheld cameras doesn't automatically guarantee better, more impassioned performances. But depending on the material, this shooting style might complement the electricity of the subject matter.

Authenticity

Two Days, One Night
2014
Cinematography:
Alain Marcoen;
directors: Jean-Pierre
and Luc Dardenne;
actor: Marion Cotillard

In *Two Days, One Night*, award-winning actress Marion Cotillard plays Sandra, who finds herself in a terrible position: In order to keep her slated-to-be-eliminated job, she must convince her coworkers to vote to give up the bonuses they would receive if she was made redundant. Written and directed with the usual rigor by brothers Jean-Pierre and Luc Dardenne, this straightforward drama follows Sandra as she goes from home to home, begging colleagues to let her keep her job.

The Dardennes often utilize handheld cameras, and *Two Days, One Night* is an excellent example of why the technique can be so effective. The storytelling is unadorned, and Cotillard gives a stripped-down, unfussy performance. The film exudes an air of authenticity, and the muted handheld photography accentuates the unvarnished realism. The camera doesn't jerk and bounce excessively, but there's enough movement of the frame that it resembles the way we take in a situation in real life, moving our head or readjusting our position to get a better view. The filmmakers' camerawork is subtle but powerful.

Terror

The Blair Witch Project
1999
Cinematography:
Neal Fredericks;
directors: Daniel Myrick
and Eduardo Sánchez;
actor: Heather Donahue

The Blair Witch Project helped popularize the horror subgenre commonly known as "found footage": The conceit was that the film we're watching is compiled from material shot by the subjects themselves. Hits like *Cloverfield* and *Paranormal Activity* owe a debt to *The Blair Witch Project*, which wielded handheld cameras to create the illusion of reality. Viewers were terrified because they were willing to believe that what they were watching was "real."

It's important to point out that this 1999 smash – which features a group of documentary filmmakers, including Heather (Heather Donahue), investigating a local legend – wasn't scary simply because of handheld cameras. By mimicking the look of nonfiction films (and advertising itself as a documentary), *The Blair Witch Project* removed the safe distance between the viewer and the material. Because we weren't sure if this was "only a movie," the horror felt unfiltered, more immediate.

Audiences have become accustomed to found-footage horror films, so the novelty of their terrors isn't as fresh as it once was. But aspiring storytellers should keep in mind that handheld shooting can erase the appearance of fiction in their work. Instead, there is only the appearance of reality, where anything is possible.

POV Shot

Letting the audience see the world through a character's eyes

We observe everything around us from our perspective, literally. Our eyes provide an entry point into the world, giving us a unique visual point of view that no one else has. In movies, the camera's lens is the viewer's eye, and often that perspective is not that of a character in the story. But occasionally, the camera becomes a specific individual's visual viewpoint, and so we see the story from his or her exact angle and height.

This is known as a POV (point-of-view) shot, which can be popular in horror movies (there are few things more frightening than realizing that we're seeing the serial killer's next unsuspecting victim through his eyes). This type of shot gives us a novel way of absorbing the information in a scene, whether it's in a drama, an action flick or a found-footage monster movie.

Relating to a character

The Diving Bell and the Butterfly
2007
Cinematography: Janusz Kamiński; director: Julian Schnabel; actor: Emmanuelle Seigner

A POV shot can be an effective tool for allowing an audience to understand your protagonist's mindset. Instead of asking viewers to walk a mile in his shoes, we simply see the world through his eyes. That's especially true with *The Diving Bell and the Butterfly*, which tells the true story of Jean-Dominique Bauby (Mathieu Amalric), a writer and editor who develops locked-in syndrome, forced to communicate with the world by blinking one eye.

Director Julian Schnabel and cinematographer Janusz Kamiński incorporate POV shots so that we realize just how frightening it was for Bauby to adjust to this potentially restrictive new life. Seeing through the character's eyes, we notice how blurry and distorted his eyesight is. We feel his physical restrictions in a visceral way.

"It's very seldom that you have a story that allows for this kind of alteration of the image," Kamiński told *MovieMaker* in 2008. "Our character has impaired vision, and he's coming out of unconsciousness. He fantasizes and has flashbacks, and he's using his imagination to survive. All this creates tremendous visual opportunities."

As a result, we feel closer to Bauby than we might in a more traditionally shot biopic. The viewer sees the people who are close to him, including his wife Céline (Emmanuelle Seigner), with a passion, intimacy and perspective that's intensely personal. We share his experience and suffer with him as he tries to rebuild his life.

Bringing the horror closer

Cloverfield
2008
Cinematography:
Michael Bonvillain;
director: Matt Reeves

Found-footage horror films use faux-authenticity to bring more suspense and realism to the scares. *Cloverfield* is part of the genre, but its innovation is that everything we see was shot by one of the characters, Hud (T.J. Miller), on a camcorder. In the film, what started as a going-away party quickly morphs into a terrifying chronicling of a monster attack in New York City, and Hud films the entire ordeal while making frightened commentary along the way.

In other words, we're "seeing" *Cloverfield* through Hud's eyes. Director Matt Reeves isn't necessarily trying to create a tight relationship between the character and us. Rather, the film presents the horror from an "unfiltered" perspective: We're up close as everything happens. There's no escape for the viewer, just as there seems to be no way out for the characters as they run for their lives. This filming technique removes the safety we might otherwise feel during a more conventional horror movie. What the characters see, we see at the same moment.

Making us the hero

Hardcore Henry
2015
Cinematography:
Vsevolod Kaptur, Fedor
Lyass and Pasha Kapinos;
director: Ilya Naishuller

There's a tradition in video games of what's known as "first-person shooters," which is a type of game in which everything is seen through the eyes of the main character. *Hardcore Henry* brought that approach to cinema.

In the movie, a mysterious man named Henry goes on an outrageous adventure: After waking up in a strange location, he discovers he has no memory of what has occurred, who he is, how he got there, or why people are out to kill him. However, *Hardcore Henry*'s conceit is that Henry is "you," meaning the viewer. Everything that happens in the film is from "Henry's" perspective. In essence, we are the star of the movie.

By strapping a GoPro to the camera operator, who performed as "Henry," director Ilya Naishuller sought to bring a new level of excitement and intensity to an action movie. Admittedly, this is an extreme experiment, but it illustrates how POV shots make us feel like a movie isn't just happening to "them" up there on the screen. By becoming Henry, we are the story's central focus. The other characters speak directly to us, and we run, shoot, jump and fall during the action sequences. We get to live vicariously through the character – without having to worry about getting hurt.

Split Diopter

Fashioning a clever visual trick to create tension

Have you ever been watching a scene in a movie in which two different areas of the screen are in focus simultaneously? It's a jarring but also striking effect, and it's executed by using a split diopter. And it doesn't take much effort to achieve. By applying an additional lens on top of the primary lens, you essentially have two lenses for the same shot, each able to focus on a different plane in the frame.

This may sound a little like deep focus, which we've already discussed, but here's the crucial difference: Not everything in the frame in a split diopter shot is in focus. As cinematographer Gordon Willis once explained, "You're altering the focal length of the lens somewhat. It's like these bifocals I have here; with these glasses you have one strength to read and another strength to see out in the distance."

Consequently, these shots can unsettle us because they don't closely mimic what the human eye sees on its own. And, as we'll discuss here, that's entirely the point.

Activity

All the President's Men
1976
Cinematography:
Gordon Willis; director:
Alan J. Pakula; actor:
Robert Redford

When cinematographer Gordon Willis was approached by frequent collaborator, director Alan J. Pakula, to shoot the true-life newspaper thriller *All the President's Men*, he knew the complicated job ahead of him. "[It was] to be a deep-focus movie because of everything that was going on," he once recalled. "There were times, in order to make that idea work, we applied diopters to hold people in the foreground as well as in the background."

Willis pointed to a crucial scene in the film, which follows *Washington Post* reporters Carl Bernstein (Dustin Hoffman) and Bob Woodward (Robert Redford) as they investigate who authorized the Watergate break-in of 1972. In the shot, Woodward is engaged in an important telephone conversation, interviewing a source who's giving him vital information. At the same time, his colleagues are in the background watching a television. Both items are in sharp focus.

Why do this? *All the President's Men* adeptly illustrates how a newsroom is a constant swirl of motion and chatter, and so by keeping the background in focus, Pakula reminds us that Woodward is far from alone in this loud, hectic space. There's electricity in the scene because of what the reporter is learning, but there's additional energy in the framing because of what's going on around him.

Passion

The Untouchables
1987
Cinematography: Stephen H. Burum; director: Brian De Palma; actors: Sean Connery, Kevin Costner

Brian De Palma has made extensive use of split diopter in his films, and an excellent example of the technique's potential is from *The Untouchables* during a scene in which federal agent Eliot Ness (Kevin Costner) and local cop Jimmy Malone (Sean Connery) meet in a church to discuss how best to take down mobster Al Capone (Robert De Niro). This is commonly known as the "Chicago way" scene, because Jimmy explains to Eliot how things are handled in the Windy City: "Here's how you get Capone: He pulls a knife, you pull a gun. He sends one of yours to the hospital, you send one of *his* to the morgue. *That's* the Chicago way!"

The punchy dialogue by David Mamet amplifies the drama, but so does De Palma's choice to use a split diopter. Working with cinematographer Stephen H. Burum, De Palma ensures that both men are in focus so that we fully absorb each character's reactions. The scene is about Jimmy trying to convince Eliot that he has to play dirtier than might be comfortable – he's drawing the younger man into ethically murky terrain. The split diopter creates a dizzying effect comparable to how Eliot feels as he questions how far he's willing to go to stop Capone.

Dynamism

The Hateful Eight
2015
Cinematography:
Robert Richardson;
director: Quentin
Tarantino; actors:
Walton Goggins,
Samuel L. Jackson

Making a movie that takes place mostly in a lodge creates logistical problems, including how to shoot the space in such a way that it doesn't become too monotonous. Quentin Tarantino and director of photography Robert Richardson responded to this visual challenge in *The Hateful Eight* by utilizing split diopter shots to tell the story of a group of desperate characters (including Samuel L. Jackson, Kurt Russell and Jennifer Jason Leigh) who become engaged in an increasingly tense showdown.

The technique helps to complicate our rooting interests. There are no clear good guys in *The Hateful Eight*, just differing degrees of moral rot, and by keeping different characters in focus in each shot, Tarantino advises us to keep our eye on all the participants. The shots crank up the tension between the characters, and when things start to get bloody later in the film, the split diopter enhances the disconcerting tone. There's nowhere to escape from these poor bastards, who are all cooped up in the same claustrophobic space.

Split Screen

Reorienting the viewer to consider multiple scenes or images simultaneously

Split screen is a technique that's been wielded by generations of filmmakers, but perhaps its most famous practitioner is Brian De Palma, so we'll use a quote he gave to *The New York Times* in 2013 to explain its power: "The thing about split screen is: It's a kind of meditative form. You can go very slowly with it, because there's a lot to look at. People are making juxtapositions in their mind."

As De Palma suggests, split screen requires our brains to process visual information in ways we normally don't when we're watching a film. This cinematic device can be incorporated for lots of reasons, but to keep things simple we'll cite three examples from different films to illustrate possible advantages of split screens.

A new way to show a familiar scene

Scott Pilgrim vs. the World
2010
Cinematography: Bill
Pope; director: Edgar
Wright; actors: Anna
Kendrick, Michael Cera

As its name implies, split screen is when the frame is divided into segments, with different characters or scenes presented in each mini-frame. 2010's *Scott Pilgrim vs. the World* makes extensive use of split screens, in part, to mimic the look of comic books, which divide each page into different frames or moments. But this still, which features Stacey (Anna Kendrick) and her brother Scott (Michael Cera) having a phone conversation, demonstrates the simplest reason why split screen can be effective.

Ordinarily, a phone call in a film is an excuse to unload some exposition – one character is telling another character information he or she might need – and the director will cut between one speaker and the other. Instead, filmmaker Edgar Wright shows them both on the screen simultaneously. As a result, we get a different experience of a phone call. We see their reactions, and they both feel like active participants, rather than individuals who bat the conversation back and forth. Plus, it's a more dynamic way of presenting the information that will be dispensed in the scene, adding some visual pop.

An opportunity to hint at a spark between characters

Down with Love
2003
Cinematography:
Jeff Cronenweth;
director: Peyton Reed;
actors: Renée Zellweger,
Ewan McGregor

2003's *Down with Love* gives us an illustration of how a split screen can add sexual tension to a scene. The characters may not be in the same location, but the device brings them together in suggestive ways.

The film pairs a strong-willed author, Barbara (Renée Zellweger), and a womanizer, Catcher (Ewan McGregor), and then sits back to watch the sparks fly. Director Peyton Reed pays homage to older romantic comedies such as *Pillow Talk*, which used split screens as a way to imply intimacy that otherwise couldn't be shown on-screen for fear of running afoul of cultural norms at the time. *Down with Love* copies the technique, and so we have scenes of Barbara and Catcher flirting while talking on the phone. As in those bygone Rock Hudson/Doris Day films, a split screen serves as a slight buffer between the potential lovebirds, almost a cinematic chaperone that ensures nothing untoward can happen between them.

Of course, Reed is being cheeky – cultural norms are far more relaxed in the twenty-first century than they were 60 years ago – but a split screen can imply the closeness between characters, even if they're in completely different rooms or cities or continents.

A broader perspective on the action

Timecode
2000
Cinematography: Patrick Alexander Stewart; director: Mike Figgis; actors: Salma Hayek, Jeanne Tripplehorn, Stellan Skarsgård, Saffron Burrows

Our final example is from the 2000 experimental drama *Timecode*, which was written and directed by Oscar-nominated *Leaving Las Vegas* filmmaker Mike Figgis. *Timecode* is an ensemble piece constructed by having four camera operators film simultaneously the story's actions in real time. The viewer sees what the operators shot as four different frames on the screen, essentially allowing the audience to choose what to pay attention to at any point in the story.

Figgis's ploy may have been little more than a gimmick – *Timecode* didn't inspire many to follow its example – but it remains a fascinating exercise. For one thing, the film reminds viewers that just because a character drops out of the central narrative, that doesn't mean she's no longer walking around in the world. Split screen allows us to check in on different individuals, inviting audiences to draw invisible connections between the core storyline and what's happening on the periphery.

If nothing else, *Timecode* is a challenge to filmmakers to expand the possibilities of telling multiple stories at the same time. Splitting the screen can mean splitting up a narrative as well, creating space for mini-tales and intriguing digressions from the principal story. As with others who have incorporated the technique, Figgis encourages us to think differently about how a frame can be constructed.

Zoom

Drawing the viewer closer to the action – or moving away for a provocative purpose

The camera move known as zooming is unique because, unlike other cinematic techniques, it doesn't exactly mimic how the human eye works. We ourselves can't "zoom in" or "zoom out" the way a camera can. (In either case, the operator is manipulating the lens's focal length, as opposed to moving the camera itself.)

However, as we'll see, a zoom can replicate a sensation that we have when we want to get a closer look at something shocking or confusing. But unlike you and me, who would simply move toward what we want to see, the camera lens itself zooms in, providing us with greater detail of the crucial visual information. Because zooms don't match the function of the human eye, they can be a little strange for the viewer. But that strangeness is often precisely the filmmaker's intention – he or she wants us to be provoked because something dramatic is about to happen.

Shock

McCabe & Mrs. Miller
1971
Cinematography:
Vilmos Zsigmond;
director: Robert Altman;
actors: Keith Carradine,
Manfred Schulz

Robert Altman frequently used zooms in his movies. "The zoom is a great help when dealing with actors," he once said. "You can't lie to them or even fool them ... But with a zoom, no one was quite sure what was happening. I could get a tight close-up from 100 feet away."

The director often sought a laidback, lifelike vibe in classics such as *Nashville* and *Short Cuts*, and zooming gave audiences a sense that we were eavesdropping on the action as it was spontaneously unfolding in front of us. Of course, that seeming spontaneity was carefully designed, as is masterfully demonstrated in Altman's revisionist Western *McCabe & Mrs. Miller*.

In this scene, an unnamed cowboy played by Keith Carradine discovers that he's walked into danger when he's confronted by a cold-blooded killer (Manfred Schulz) who asks to see the man's gun. When the cowboy complies, the killer uses the opportunity as an excuse to shoot him dead. Altman and cinematographer Vilmos Zsigmond strikingly zoom in as the cowboy plunges into the icy water below the bridge where he'd once been standing. The camera move imitates our desire to move closer to see such a horrifying sight. *McCabe & Mrs. Miller* later zooms in even closer, almost as if the lens can't believe what's occurred. The zooming magnifies our shock, forcing us to contend with this tragic turn of events.

Electricity

Star Wars: The Force Awakens
2015
Cinematography:
Dan Mindel; director:
J.J. Abrams

Filmmakers such as Edgar Wright and Quentin Tarantino enjoy utilizing what's known as whip zooms, snap zooms or crash zooms. The different names all refer to the same technique, which, as their colorful monikers should indicate, is an abrupt, sudden camera move. Rather than the deliberate zooms used by Altman, these hurtle us from one perspective to a closer one. A whip zoom is self-consciously hectic, almost unsteady, and we're meant to feel the electricity of the move. It's intentionally dynamic and showy.

J.J. Abrams is also a fan of whip zooms, which appear in his action sequences, memorably in *The Force Awakens* during a high-flying chase scene between our heroes in the Millennium Falcon and the evil pilots of the First Order. At one point, Abrams shows us an exterior shot of the Falcon being pursued by TIE fighters, and when Rey (Daisy Ridley) steers the ship inside a downed Star Destroyer, the camera quickly whip zooms to give us a closer look, almost as if this detail of the wider shot has been enhanced and enlarged.

It's worth noting that this sequence was rendered digitally – neither the Millennium Falcon nor the TIE fighters is real, of course – but Abrams is nonetheless drawing from organic camera techniques to goose our excitement level. The Falcon is moving so fast that we need a whip zoom to keep up.

Discovery

Quiz Show
1994
Cinematography:
Michael Ballhaus;
director: Robert Redford;
actor: Ralph Fiennes

In the Oscar-nominated *Quiz Show*, director Robert Redford uses a specific type of zoom called the dolly zoom (or zolly), in which the camera pushes back while the lens zooms in. (Alternately, the camera can be pushed forward while the lens zooms out.) Why execute these two seemingly contradictory movements at the same time? Because, while the subject at the center of your frame stays relatively the same, the background changes noticeably. We are no longer looking at a seemingly ordinary scene – something surreal is occurring right in front of our eyes.

Redford incorporates a dolly zoom during a crucial scene in the film, which is about the corruption that went on behind the scenes of the popular 1950s game show *Twenty-One*: A good-looking, charismatic contestant, Charles Van Doren (Ralph Fiennes), was given the answers in advance in order to ensure that he'd keep winning and appearing on the program, thus boosting its ratings. This scene shows the moment that Van Doren receives an answer through his headphones. Redford could have simply provided the audio that went along with the cheating, but the dolly zoom makes the cheating feel more dramatic and abhorrent. The image itself is disorienting, just as Van Doren's treachery defies the rules of fairness that a show like *Twenty-One* ought to uphold.

EDITING

Dissolve, Wipe and Fade

Finding myriad creative ways to move from one scene to another

Let's briefly discuss a few different ways to transition between scenes. Dissolves and fades are frequently utilized by editors to insert a little mood into a transition, while wipes are less common (we'll explain why shortly).

A dissolve is when one image "dissolves" into the other, almost as if the first image is evaporating in order to reveal the second. Fades are also called "fade to black," which means that the image grows increasingly darker until it's entirely black. And in a wipe, the first image is literally "wiped away" by the introduction of the second image, not unlike the way a squeegee wipes the water, soap or dirt off a windshield.

None of these transitional devices is superior (or inferior) to the others – and there's nothing wrong with simply using traditional edits. It's merely a question of how you want to convey certain tones or ideas between scenes. Sometimes, how you move from one scene to another is as important as the scenes themselves.

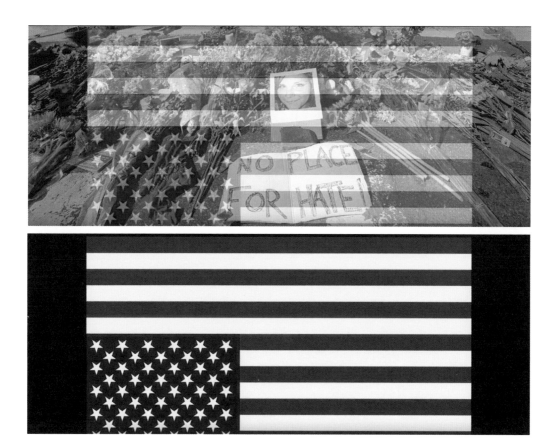

Dissolve

BlacKkKlansman
2018
Editing: Barry Alexander
Brown; director: Spike Lee

Spike Lee's Oscar-winning film tells the incredible true story of a 1970s Black cop (John David Washington) working in an all-white police force in Colorado who cleverly infiltrated a local Ku Klux Klan. But Lee doesn't want the film to simply be a period piece – rather, he is drawing connections between the past and the present, showing how white supremacy and racism are as much an element of our times as they were decades ago.

To illustrate this point, Lee ends *BlacKkKlansman* with devastating footage of a 2017 alt-right rally in Charlottesville, Virginia, that turned violent, leading to the murder of an innocent bystander, Heather Heyer. Lee powerfully dissolves from a still image of Heyer to a collection of flowers left where she was fatally struck by a neo-Nazi's car. The filmmaker then dissolves from that image to one of an upside-down American flag – a distress signal – that changes from red, white and blue to mournful black and white.

These two dissolves amplify the tragedy and horror of what Lee is depicting. Heyer's death was a sobering symbol of the bigotry still consuming America, and the editing technique allows us to fully absorb the senselessness of her death and the deeper implications for the country in general.

Wipe

Star Wars
1977
Editing: Paul Hirsch,
Richard Chew, Marcia
Lucas; director: George
Lucas; actors: Alec
Guinness, Mark Hamill

For *Star Wars*, writer–director George Lucas decided to make extensive use of wipes between scenes in homage to a childhood influence, 1940's *Flash Gordon Conquers the Universe*, which incorporates them frequently. The device helped add to the film's fairytale-like quality, enhancing the sense that this space odyssey was a fantastical, old-fashioned adventure. To perpetuate this sensation, the *Star Wars* sequels and prequels also incorporate wipes. Beyond the beloved, familiar characters and John Williams's iconic score, those wipes help establish that we're watching a *Star Wars* film.

However, wipes are so synonymous with Lucas's popular franchise that you rarely see them in other movies. In fact, wipes are not featured in the *Star Wars* spin-offs, such as *Rogue One*, in order to signal that those movies are not part of the central storyline. During the promotion of *Rogue One*, producer Kathleen Kennedy said as much: "The *Star Wars* saga films have a responsibility to maintain a continuity of tone and stylistic device. Things like the crawl at the beginning, and the wipes. But with the standalone films we're relaxing some of those rules so that we can try stylistic and tonal experiments that depart from what we've seen."

Wipes are certainly a dynamic way of cutting between scenes, but for many viewers, the cinematic technique is too closely tied to those sci-fi blockbusters that took place a long time ago in a galaxy far, far away.

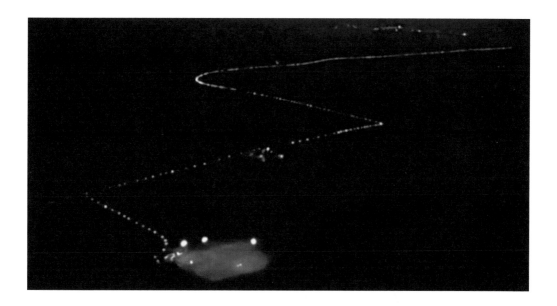

Fade

Field of Dreams
1989
Editing: Ian Crafford;
director: Phil Alden
Robinson

Fades occur at different points in movies, often to suggest that, even though we're not going to see the rest of a scene, we can guess what will happen. (For instance, sex scenes fade to black before the risqué moments take place.) A fade can also indicate that we'll be moving forward in time – the fade-out is almost like taking a breath to prepare us for the temporal shift.

For our purposes, though, we're going to focus on fades being used at the end of a film. It's clichéd to conclude a story with the sentence, "And they all lived happily ever after," but a fade can, in essence, communicate the same sentiment. The fade is a gentle indicator to the audience that the story is over and that everything will work out great for the main characters.

Field of Dreams demonstrates this use of a fade-out. At the film's conclusion, Kevin Costner's Ray is enjoying a catch with his father (Dwier Brown) while, in the distance, rows of cars are driving toward his magical baseball diamond. All of *Field of Dreams*'s central conflicts have been resolved: Ray has made peace with his dad; his family will not have to sell their home; and the baseball diamond will bring in massive business. As the movie ends, director Phil Alden Robinson quietly fades out, capping this sentimental tale on a heartwarming note. The fade becomes a comforting reassurance. We know all is well.

Smash Cut

Juxtaposing one image with another, shocking the viewer in the process

"Smash cut" is a violent term to describe an editing technique that's meant to disrupt the viewer. As opposed to a typical edit, which smoothly moves us from one scene or shot to the next, a smash cut intentionally startles or provokes. There are myriad reasons to do this, but to grossly simplify, the filmmaker wants us to notice the juxtaposition between the two shots and draw conclusions about why they've been paired in such a surprising way.

Here, we will look at three of the most iconic smash cuts in film history. Even after decades of close study and endless cultural homages, they retain their power to shock or amuse. Not every smash cut needs to be this extreme, but these illustrate the possibilities of adventurous editing choices.

A dazzling new locale

Lawrence of Arabia
1962
Editing: Anne V. Coates;
director: David Lean;
actor: Peter O'Toole

Early in this biopic of T.E. Lawrence (Peter O'Toole), the young British officer accepts an assignment to be relocated from Cairo to Arabia, which represents a fresh start for this directionless, immature man. But rather than simply cutting from one location to another, Oscar-winning director David Lean and editor Anne V. Coates do something radical. In one shot, Lawrence is watching a match burn down. But as he gets ready to blow it out, we then cut to the rising sun in the desert. In essence, Lawrence "blew out" the one shot and brought us into the next.

It's an extremely clever smash cut, but it also serves a narrative purpose. Before the cut, a diplomat (Claude Rains) warns Lawrence about how brutal the desert can be ("For ordinary men, it's a burning fiery furnace"). The next shot quietly illustrates what a scorching environment Lawrence will be entering. As viewers, we feel as if we've been yanked from the luxury of Lawrence's previous locale and thrust into an uninviting new realm. Lean and Coates welcome us into this dazzling new world – but it's one that will greatly test our hero's mettle.

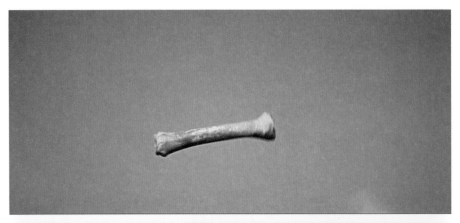

A mammoth
time jump

2001: A Space Odyssey
1968
Editing: Ray Lovejoy;
director: Stanley Kubrick

In *2001*, director Stanley Kubrick imagines humanity's evolution from simple primates to, in the film's transcendent conclusion, a luminous Star Child. Early on, the movie makes a startling leap forward in time from "The Dawn of Man" to a future in which humans can easily travel from Earth to the Moon on commercial spaceships. To mark this temporal transition, Kubrick and editor Ray Lovejoy cut from an ape throwing a bone into the air to an orbiting spacecraft circling our planet.

There are a few thematic links between the two shots. For one thing, the bone and the spacecraft are similarly shaped, and both are airborne. But also, Kubrick is asking us to consider how both objects, in their own way, are simply tools used to help people. The bone was a primitive weapon, while the spacecraft is a higher-tech instrument wielded by humans eons later.

But the stark contrast between the two images, and the two locations, helps to underline Kubrick's main narrative objective, which is to visualize just how far ahead in time we've jumped. Dynamically, *2001* informs us that we're now entering a new era, while inviting us to consider how, despite the flash-forward in years, human beings remain fundamentally the same: distrustful, competitive, inquisitive, hopelessly restrained by the limits of our technology and knowledge. *2001*'s smash cut is quick, but its intellectual impact lingers.

A wonderful innuendo

North by Northwest
1959
Editing: George Tomasini;
director: Alfred Hitchcock;
actors: Cary Grant, Eva
Marie Saint

Arguably Alfred Hitchcock's most purely entertaining film, *North by Northwest* is the tale of an innocent man, Roger Thornhill (Cary Grant), who gets caught up in a deadly spy game after he's mistaken for another man. Along the way, he befriends a beautiful stranger, Eve Kendall (Eva Marie Saint), who might be part of the conspiracy.

Indicative of its sexy and playful tone, *North by Northwest* features two smash cuts near the end. In the first, Eve is hanging on for dear life at the edge of Mount Rushmore. Roger offers his hand to pull her up, and as he does, we smash cut to him helping her into a bed in a train car. We've gone from one location to another – and from a moment of high tension to a warm, romantic scene. We didn't see him rescue her, but we surmise that it occurred during the cut.

But then another smash cut awaits us. As the lovers kiss deeply, reclining on the bed together in the midst of their passionate embrace, Hitchcock and editor George Tomasini cut to an exterior shot of the train speeding into a tunnel. What's being communicated here? *North by Northwest* is slyly alluding to what will soon be happening between Roger and Eve, using a phallic train entering a tunnel to symbolize their ensuing intercourse. No one said all smash cuts had to be intellectual exercises. Some of them are just cheeky and a touch naughty.

Crosscutting

Moving between action in different locations, juggling suspense on several fronts

An individual sequence can be suspenseful, but what if it was combined with another equally suspenseful sequence that was occurring in another location – or another time period? This is the general idea behind crosscutting, in which a filmmaker moves between locales, linking them in the viewer's mind.

Sometimes, that linking is meant to create an odd juxtaposition. (Perhaps the most famous example of this is in *The Godfather*, where a baby's baptism is crosscut with a mob hit, the thematic link being that Al Pacino's Michael Corleone is orchestrating each event.) But the overriding strategy is that, by crosscutting the sequences, the impact will be greater than the sum of the individual parts. The effect can be dizzying or provocative.

An action sequence, in three parts

Return of the Jedi
1983
Editing: Sean Barton, Marcia Lucas, Duwayne Dunham; director: Richard Marquand; actors: David Prowse, Mark Hamill, Harrison Ford, Carrie Fisher

For the grand finale of the original *Star Wars* trilogy, we're treated to an action sequence that takes place in three different locales, all tied together. In the first, Luke Skywalker (Mark Hamill) squares off with Darth Vader (voiced by James Earl Jones) aboard the Death Star. In the second, Han Solo (Harrison Ford) and Princess Leia (Carrie Fisher) lead a team of Rebellion fighters, who are on Endor. Finally, there's a massive battle in outer space around the Death Star.

Director Richard Marquand crosscuts between these three locales, giving us a series of cliffhangers. Each individual sequence builds in suspense, as our heroes look like they're going to fail in their separate missions. Everywhere that Marquand takes us, we're rooting for the Rebellion but fearful that the Empire will finally reign triumphant. Any one of these sequences would be enthralling enough. When they're strung together, however, we get a greater sense of all the people involved – and the life-or-death stakes of the entire trilogy. As a result, when the good guys vanquish their foes, we get the satisfaction three times over.

To conclude one of Hollywood's most iconic trilogies, the filmmakers had to do something extra. Marquand's ambitious crosscutting fits the bill.

An intertwining fate

Cloud Atlas
2012
Editing: Alexander Berner; directors: Lana and Lilly Wachowski and Tom Tykwer; actor: Tom Hanks

"Everything Is Connected" reads the tagline for *Cloud Atlas*, which looked at a series of characters across different periods of human history. Intriguingly, the Wachowskis and Tom Tykwer decided to cast the same actors to play different characters, underlining novelist David Mitchell's argument that our fates are intertwined in ways we cannot appreciate.

In the film, Tom Hanks plays, among others, Henry Goose (a nineteenth-century doctor), Dermot Hoggins (a twenty-first-century author), and Zachry (a twenty-fourth-century warrior). He's one of many sets of characters in *Cloud Atlas*, which also features stars like Ben Whishaw and Halle Berry in multiple roles. The filmmakers never focus on just one time period, or one character. Instead, we move across centuries back and forth, and the crosscutting seeks to emphasize eternal recurrence – a belief in our common humanity and inter-connectedness, and the fact that certain events occur again and again over time.

The only way to truly make these points would be through crosscutting. If we are to understand how linked we are, we need to see the similarities between the characters in *Cloud Atlas*. Even though the film spans hundreds of years, the crosscutting erases that mammoth time period. We're invited to notice how alike these different characters are, even if they aren't alive at the same time.

One war, several individual battles

Dunkirk
2017
Editing: Lee Smith;
director: Christopher
Nolan; actors: James
D'Arcy, Kenneth Branagh,
Tom Hardy, Mark Rylance

Christopher Nolan's 2017 war film takes us to 1940, when British and Allied troops are trying to evacuate from Northern France as German troops descend upon them. *Dunkirk* dramatizes the event by showing us several individual scenes, each of them utterly nerve-racking. In one, Commander Bolton (Kenneth Branagh) tries to help his stranded soldiers find safe passage back to England. The second involves a pilot (Tom Hardy) engaged in dogfights with enemy planes. And then there's Dawson (Mark Rylance), a civilian who steers his private boat into danger in order to help rescue British servicemen.

Lee Smith won the Oscar for Best Editing, brilliantly weaving these different sequences together. Although the time period for the individual narrative pieces varies – some last a week, others just an hour – the crosscutting allows them to coexist in a thrilling whole. *Dunkirk* is a flurry of sensation and horror, and Smith's deft editing illustrates how all these men are fighting for the same cause, although many of them aren't aware of the individuals in the other sequences.

There aren't a lot of deeply developed characters in *Dunkirk*, but Nolan isn't after that. Instead, he's honoring the collective spirit of soldiers fighting against tyranny. Crosscutting adds immeasurable emotional oomph to Nolan's formal strategy.

Jump Cut

Disorienting the viewer by chopping up scenes and ignoring the rules of continuity

In life, we don't suddenly jump ahead a few seconds or minutes. But in film editing, you can. A jump cut involves a transition, normally within the same scene, that doesn't flow smoothly from what we just saw. Where traditional cuts take us to a different angle of the same scene so that we see it from a different perspective, a jump cut is often from the same camera angle. The effect is willfully disorienting.

Documentaries often involve jump cuts because, as opposed to fiction films, there's no audience presumption that what we're seeing will follow the rules of "proper" filmmaking (reality rarely obeys such orderly rules). So, for example, a talking-head interview might feature the occasional jump cut as the director chooses specific moments from the longer conversation that are the most important. But because the interview was all filmed from the same angle, it looks like the person "jumps" from one shot to the next.

Let's examine how jump cuts can be wielded in narrative storytelling, either to heighten a mood or challenge cinematic conventions.

Provocation

Breathless
1960
Editing: Cécile Decugis;
director: Jean-Luc Godard;
actor: Jean Seberg

Of course, no discussion of jump cuts would be complete without mentioning *Breathless*, the groundbreaking film from director Jean-Luc Godard. In this French New Wave classic, Michel (Jean-Paul Belmondo) and Patricia (Jean Seberg) are Parisian lovers who seem disaffected and aimless. Michel imitates Humphrey Bogart and is a small-time crook, until he shoots a police officer and finds himself in serious trouble. Patricia wants to be a journalist, and although she has affection for Michel – and may be carrying his child – she doesn't seem particularly perturbed by the possibility that he might be a killer.

In other words, these are characters who don't adhere to the strictures of what main characters "should" do: They're not particularly sympathetic or proactive. This is all part of Godard's design, which deconstructs genres, filmic influences and narrative convention. Likewise, he eschews traditional editing, impulsively jumping forward in scenes. He'll film one of his actors from one angle and then cut to later in the exchange, but from the same angle. This strategy calls attention to all the assumptions we make about films. We take it for granted that they'll be "professionally" edited. *Breathless* shatters that assumption, along with dozens of others.

Intensity

The Royal Tenenbaums
2001
Editing: Dylan Tichenor;
director: Wes Anderson;
actor: Luke Wilson

Wes Anderson's bittersweet comedy about a flailing family mostly mines melancholic laughs. But in its darkest moment, *The Royal Tenenbaums* harrowingly depicts Richie Tenenbaum's (Luke Wilson) descent into bottomless grief once he learns that his true love, Margot (Gwyneth Paltrow), has been hiding several secrets. Inconsolable, Richie shaves off his beard and then slits his wrists.

It's a shocking moment in an otherwise funny film, and Anderson hints at its traumatic nature by incorporating jump cuts. The rationale is obvious but shrewd: As opposed to the rest of this precisely shot and scripted movie, the sequence feels unhinged and frantic. We are getting a glimpse inside Richie's head as the character is quickly unraveling. A desperate mental state is depicted visually in stunning ways.

Anxiety

Melancholia
2011
Editing: Molly Malene
Stensgaard; director:
Lars von Trier; actors:
Alexander Skarsgård,
Kirsten Dunst

Lars von Trier often uses jump cuts. It seems that there are a few reasons for this. The first is that it's part of a general aesthetic that he prefers in his filmmaking, which is to emphasize a rough, handmade quality (keep in mind he often films with handheld cameras). But jump cuts in seemingly banal scenes also inject an air of anxiety into his movies. Early on in *Melancholia*, Justine (Kirsten Dunst) and Michael (Alexander Skarsgård) are enjoying their wedding day. This should, in theory, be a happy moment, but because Von Trier inserts jump cuts, we feel some uncertainty. The lack of "proper" cuts from one scene to the next leaves us on edge.

This technique can be overdone, of course, and so a filmmaker needs to be careful how often and why jump cuts are introduced. Von Trier's movies are an excellent example of how to use them intuitively. Watch his films and you'll notice that jump cuts give his work a peculiar but potent rhythm. Von Trier often examines the darkest parts of human nature, and so jump cuts make a certain amount of narrative sense. In his world, society is often collapsing into chaos. How better to show that collapse than anxiously cutting his shots to shreds?

Non-diegetic Sound

Allowing the audience to hear things that the characters cannot – or, why a musical score matters

Every day, we're surrounded by sounds. People talking. Music blasting from a passing car. Birds squawking. Dogs barking. The wind blowing through the trees. In movies, characters hear all those things – but a film also contains a whole other set of sounds that the people up on the screen *don't* hear. Those are for the audience. It's known as non-diegetic sound.

A film's score is part of its non-diegetic sound. If characters speak in voiceover, that's also non-diegetic sound. The easiest way to distinguish what qualifies is that it's any sort of sound, noise or music that exists *outside* the characters' world. Here, we'll explore the value of non-diegetic sound and the emotional undercurrents these pieces of audio add to a film.

Feel the terror

Psycho
1960
Composer: Bernard
Herrmann; director:
Alfred Hitchcock;
actor: Anthony Perkins

Oscar-winner Bernard Herrmann composed the score for *Psycho*, and like most film scores, the music is heard by the audience and not the characters in the story. Perhaps the movie's most famous bit of non-diegetic sound comes in the tragic shower scene, in which Marion Crane (Janet Leigh) is killed by Norman Bates (Anthony Perkins). When Bates pulls back the curtain and starts to stab her, we hear a screeching *eee-eee-eee-eee* noise from a violin. Neither Marion nor Norman is aware of that sound, but for the audience, it embodies the shock, violence and horror of the situation.

What Herrmann managed to achieve was to articulate the feeling of terror in a single, repeated sound. That moment of non-diegetic sound is so synonymous with *Psycho* that simply hearing the song elsewhere, your mind immediately goes back to Marion's death. Additionally, Herrmann's score has become ubiquitous in the culture, with people mimicking that noise to suggest a lethal killing. This is the power of non-diegetic sound – it becomes society's sonic shorthand for a particular emotion or situation.

Understand the character

Casino Royale
2006
Composer: David Arnold;
director: Martin Campbell;
actor: Daniel Craig

When you watch a James Bond movie, you will invariably hear what's officially known as "James Bond Theme," the slow, sexy, strutting music that was written by Monty Norman and arranged by John Barry. Plenty of film characters have their own theme music, and 007's is a good example of what this type of non-diegetic sound can do for an audience.

For one thing, it doesn't matter who plays James Bond. "James Bond Theme" helps confer upon the actor the character's key attributes simply through music. Audiences haven't just forged a relationship with this dashing spy – we connect the music to the man: Both are stylish and suave, hinting at a little danger and intrigue. None of us is as cool as James Bond, but when that music plays, we become him, if only vicariously. None of the people on-screen hears that theme, but it communicates his vibe perfectly.

Accentuate the emotions

Wonder Woman
2017
Composer: Rupert
Gregson-Williams;
director: Patty Jenkins;
actor: Gal Gadot

Non-diegetic sound helps direct an audience on how to react during a particular scene. Sad music will play during a sad scene, or a lighthearted score will complement a comedic scene. For *Wonder Woman*, director Patty Jenkins and composer Rupert Gregson-Williams help us understand Diana's (Gal Gadot) heroism, in part, by giving her a score that accentuates her bravery – and how we should feel about it.

When Wonder Woman runs across the battlefield during World War I, she's risking something none of the (male) mortals around her would dare, putting herself into harm's way in such a blatant manner. But she's so determined to help the Allied Forces that she's unafraid.

Gregson-Williams's score, that non-diegetic sound, becomes a sonic, emotional equivalent of the nerve Diana displays during that titanic battle sequence. As viewers, we'd be impressed enough by Diana's courage and skill, but the music gives her actions a stunning canvas. A score can be a manipulative tool, but it's also incredibly effective, especially if the music is as stirring as the characters.

WRITING

Dialogue

Perfecting the art of how your characters communicate with the world around them

Dialogue is a concept most people are familiar with. It's the lines that characters speak out loud. Some dialogue is funny, some is serious, and some simply pushes forward important plot or character information. (This kind of dialogue is known as exposition.) But no matter what kind of dialogue it is, those lines need to have a narrative purpose, avoiding on-the-nose obviousness to, instead, allude to the story's deeper themes. Like all of us, characters don't always say exactly what they're thinking, which adds extra layers of suspense and emotion to certain scenes.

This chapter won't teach you how to write sharper or more hilarious dialogue. But by examining three very different films, which incorporate three very different styles of dialogue, the hope is that you'll be able to see how much flexibility you as a dramatist have in terms of determining what comes out of your characters' mouths. When we talk in real life, there's always a reason – and what we say, often unknowingly, can reveal a lot about ourselves to others. Movie dialogue is no different.

Going for laughs and heart

When Harry Met Sally ...
1989
Screenplay: Nora Ephron;
director: Rob Reiner;
actors: Meg Ryan,
Billy Crystal

Longtime friends Harry (Billy Crystal) and Sally (Meg Ryan) were characters inspired by conversations between writer Nora Ephron and director Rob Reiner. As Ephron, who penned the screenplay for *When Harry Met Sally*, later explained, "What made this movie different was that Rob had a character who could say whatever he believed, and if I disagreed, I had Sally to say so for me." *When Harry Met Sally*'s dialogue is very funny, but it resonates, even after so many years, because the two characters' growing bond represents something elemental about men, women and the complications that arise once romantic feelings develop. The characters quip back and forth, but what they're talking about has an undercurrent of truth to it.

Plenty of comedies are simply hilarious, without any deeper societal commentary underneath. But aspiring filmmakers can learn from *When Harry Met Sally* how to craft dialogue that speaks honestly about insecurities and desires that lots of people feel – about looking for love, about being unsure if anyone will truly love you – and finding the humor in those universal sentiments.

It can also be effective to have your two main characters representing differing viewpoints. Harry insists men and women can't be friends because sex will get in the way; Sally disagrees. *When Harry Met Sally* is, in some ways, the chronicling of their debate. But because Harry and Sally are so funny and nuanced and real, we never think of the film as some theoretical position paper. The dialogue is too clever and zingy for that to happen.

Wrapping us in a mystery

The Spanish Prisoner
1997
Screenplay: David Mamet;
director: David Mamet;
actors: Campbell Scott,
Steve Martin

Writer–director David Mamet is known for his sharp, intentionally stilted dialogue. And the Pulitzer Prize-winning playwright of *Glengarry Glen Ross* is equally blunt when he breaks down his narrative process, once saying, "Every scene should be able to answer three questions: *Who wants what from whom? What happens if they don't get it? Why now?*"

Mamet's 1997 thriller *The Spanish Prisoner* illustrates his punchy way of writing, but it also illuminates his knack for peculiar dialogue. On the page, his dialogue can look weird, as if it's written in a foreign language and then badly translated into English. (Sample lines from *The Spanish Prisoner*: "We must never forget that we are human, and as humans we dream, and when we dream we dream of money." "Good people, bad people, they generally look like what they are.")

But that fortune-cookie succinctness is something of a ruse because, as we'll learn, many of the characters in *The Spanish Prisoner* seem to be hiding something. The directness of their dialogue is undercut by how cryptic their words really are. Mamet's films often involve schemes and scams, and *The Spanish Prisoner* is no different. But the characters' lines are their own kind of mystery. It's an extremely stylistic choice, but it's an option for screenwriters to consider. Rather than explaining things, the dialogue only obfuscates matters further. Even if every scene should answer Mamet's three questions, that doesn't mean the dialogue needs to make it easy for the audience to decipher those answers.

Seeking the soul within the spectacle

The Bridge on the River Kwai
1957
Screenplay: Carl Foreman and Michael Wilson; director: David Lean; actors: Alec Guinness, Sessue Hayakawa

There's an assumption that big action movies don't have a lot of great dialogue. After all, the characters mostly just say things like "Jump!" and "Look out!" when they're not busy delivering smartass quips, right? But that's not actually true: A good writer will infuse her characters with feeling and brains, even in war films and action movies. Just because audiences go for the spectacle doesn't mean they don't want terrific characters and engaging dialogue, too.

Granted, *The Bridge on the River Kwai* isn't, by modern standards, a high-octane event picture. But it's a fine example of how an epic adventure can also be rooted in character and dialogue. We can see this in many of the Oscar-winning film's sequences, but let's take a moment to focus on the battle of wills that takes place between British officer Nicholson (Alec Guinness) and Sessue Hayakawa's ruthless Japanese commander Saito. Nicholson and his men have been captured during World War II, but he refuses to bow to Saito's demands that the British officers help build his vaunted bridge. A face-off ensues, and the conflict is animated by Carl Foreman and Michael Wilson's intelligent, witty dialogue.

However, it's worth noting that the dialogue doesn't just escalate these characters' dispute. We get a sense of the two men – Nicholson's smooth confidence, Saito's growing insecurity – so that we truly understand what's driving each of them. There's spectacle in *The Bridge on the River Kwai*, but also plenty of soul and smarts.

Voiceover

Articulating the inner thoughts of characters – whether they're talking to themselves or us

What would it be like if you could read people's minds? That sounds like a science-fiction premise but, of course, we're able to do that all the time in movies thanks to voiceover, a screenwriting technique in which a character's thoughts are heard aloud on the soundtrack.

Voiceover has many possible functions in a film. For some movies, the device can add a novelistic quality to the storytelling. Other times, voiceover allows your main character to communicate directly to the audience. In every case, though, this narrative tool is meant to convey information that we wouldn't get otherwise in the film. But beware: Just because a voice is speaking to us, that doesn't mean we should blindly accept what it's saying.

A novelistic quality

Barry Lyndon
1975
Screenplay: Stanley
Kubrick; director:
Stanley Kubrick

In novels, there is often an omniscient narrator providing an outsider's or god's-eye view of the events. We don't know who this individual is, but that unseen "voice" guides us through the narrative, describing locations and individuals and putting us into the mindset of the central characters. It's a technique we don't see as often in films, but it does happen.

An intriguing example is Stanley Kubrick's *Barry Lyndon*, which is based on the William Makepeace Thackeray novel. The film is about Redmond Barry (Ryan O'Neal), an Irish youth making his way in the eighteenth century, frequently through scheming, but it's not his voice we hear on the soundtrack. That's actor Michael Hordern, who delivers an ironic voiceover, commenting on the action with a dispassionate detachment that suggests that poor Barry's fate has been predetermined and that he's powerless to change it.

The device gives *Barry Lyndon* a novelistic feel, but by approaching the narration from a specific angle, Kubrick clues us in on how to think of Barry. This is not a story of a brave young man who rises to great heights through his virtuousness – rather, it's a sardonic tale of a fool who gets his comeuppance. Hordern's voiceover clues us in to the movie's overall tone and worldview.

A direct line of communication

Goodfellas
1990
Screenplay: Martin
Scorsese and Nicholas
Pileggi; director:
Martin Scorsese;
actor: Ray Liotta

Martin Scorsese has often incorporated voiceover in his work. His period romantic drama *The Age of Innocence* features a narrator (Joanne Woodward) who comments on the proceedings. But perhaps his most famous use of voiceover is in *Goodfellas*, which tells the story of Henry Hill (Ray Liotta), a New Yorker who finds his calling by becoming part of the mob. Based on a true story, the screenplay (written by Scorsese and Nicholas Pileggi) follows along with Henry, who explains his motivations and provides context through voiceover.

Some screenwriting books and film classes will warn against using this kind of voiceover, dismissing it as a lazy shorthand. And while it's true that the device can be a crutch – dispensing exposition and offering a CliffsNotes summary of a character's mental state that could be more evocatively dramatized in other ways – our feeling is that, when used skillfully, voiceover can be just as effective a narrative tool as any other.

Goodfellas proves this point, as we gain a greater intimacy with Henry because he's talking to us. Liotta performs the voiceover like a confessional, and in a sense we're implicated along with him as we watch him commit various crimes. In our ordinary lives, we'd stay far away from a crook like Henry Hill. *Goodfellas*'s voiceover makes us a coconspirator.

The unreliable narrator

The Informant!
2009
Screenplay: Scott Z. Burns; director: Steven Soderbergh; actor: Matt Damon

Can you always trust voiceover? Let's look at *The Informant!*, the 2009 comedy-drama from director Steven Soderbergh. Based on a remarkable true story, the film features a protagonist who, as we'll learn, can be slippery when it comes to the truth. To have such an individual provide the film's voiceover becomes a fascinating exercise in how the technique can be used to deceive an audience. So often, we accept voiceover as fact. *The Informant!* marvelously subverts that assumption.

Early on, we meet Mark Whitacre (Matt Damon), an executive at a Midwestern food company who cheerfully tells us obscure facts and offers his opinions on some of his coworkers. What becomes clear quickly is that his voiceover is rambling, unfocused, more like the random thoughts we all have as we go through our day. Written by Scott Z. Burns (and based on Kurt Eichenwald's nonfiction book), *The Informant!* twists the strategy of a conventional voiceover by removing the idea that Mark is "talking" to the audience. Instead, he's talking to himself, and so we get to listen in on his inner monologue. But unlike most uses of the device, we don't feel any closer to this character by being inside his head. If anything, he's only more of a mystery.

As the plot unfolds, Mark emerges as a whistle-blower who wants to expose his company's price-fixing schemes. Such a premise prepares the viewer to expect an underdog story about the little guy taking on a powerful corporation, but *The Informant!* plays with our expectations here as well. The more time we spend with Mark – and the more we hear his puzzling voiceover – the more apparent it is that he can't be believed. And, eventually, we'll recognize that Mark isn't just a quirky, unreliable narrator – he has serious mental health problems.

Soderbergh's unusual character study illustrates how voiceover can be a powerful technique – one that illuminates but also misdirects.

Foreshadowing

Hinting early on at what's to come in the story

When we watch a movie, we think we're paying attention. But then, seemingly out of the blue, a plot twist will blindside us – except, it shouldn't have. After all, the surprise was hinted at much earlier in the narrative – maybe we just didn't notice.

Foreshadowing involves the storyteller giving the audience a sense of something they should be looking out for later in the film – a clue, you might say, of a future event. Sometimes, foreshadowing can be extremely subtle. A seemingly random piece of information is presented to us, only for it to prove to be far more important at the movie's conclusion. Other times, it's almost a dare. A character will say something ominous or cryptic, which creates a mystery for the audience to sit with as they wait to discover why this enigmatic dialogue was spoken in the first place.

Not all movies need foreshadowing, and dramatists have to be careful that they don't use the device inelegantly. But plenty of great movies have succeeded, in part, because of their superb use of foreshadowing.

A chilling callback

Vertigo
1958
Screenplay: Alec Coppel
and Samuel A. Taylor;
director: Alfred Hitchcock;
actors: Kim Novak,
James Stewart

In *Vertigo*, James Stewart plays Scottie, a retired detective coaxed into taking on a new case, which finds him unexpectedly falling in love with a mysterious, troubled blonde named Madeleine (Kim Novak), who jumps to her death from a church's bell tower (Scottie, because he suffers from vertigo, was powerless to stop her). Grieving, Scottie soon meets another woman, Judy (also Novak), who resembles Madeleine, and becomes obsessed with turning her into his lost beloved.

Those who have seen Alfred Hitchcock's psychological thriller know how it ends – with Scottie learning the truth about this deception and Judy accidentally falling to her death from that same bell tower. In *Vertigo*, foreshadowing is a key dramatic device. Early on, Scottie is unable to save his cop partner, who dies after a high fall. Now burdened with vertigo, Scottie faces a similar dilemma when Madeleine goes to the bell tower – once again, he can do nothing. The foreshadowing only becomes more powerful afterward, because it hints at the film's finale, which recreates the Madeleine sequence with Judy, resulting in a similar outcome.

Throughout, Hitchcock has hinted that a fear of heights will be the undoing of the film's characters. Only at the end do we see exactly what he means.

A cruel irony

Million Dollar Baby
2004
Screenplay: Paul Haggis;
director: Clint Eastwood;
actors: Clint Eastwood,
Hilary Swank

It's such a simple shot it would be easy to overlook: Whenever aging trainer Frankie (Clint Eastwood) consults with up-and-coming boxer Maggie (Hilary Swank) in her corner between rounds, he makes sure to put down her stool at the start of the break and then removes it before the fight resumes. During the boxing scenes, we're not spending a lot of time thinking about that particular action because we're too caught up in the drama of the fight.

But Eastwood, who also directed *Million Dollar Baby*, is foreshadowing something terrible that will eventually occur: In a later bout, he won't move her stool in time, and her opponent will sucker-punch her, resulting in Maggie's neck hitting the stool, leaving her paralyzed.

This is an example of foreshadowing that's practically invisible. Eastwood hides it by making the stool part of the background of the boxing sequences. We see him move the stool, but our mind processes it as just another ordinary activity that a character in that situation would normally do. It doesn't seem important. But as we'll soon realize, *Million Dollar Baby* has laid the groundwork all along for what was going to occur.

An invitation

The Prestige
2006
Screenplay: Jonathan
Nolan; director:
Christopher Nolan;
actor: Michael Caine

The Prestige is about two rival magicians (Christian Bale and Hugh Jackman), and the film itself is about the gamesmanship and wonder of magic tricks. In fact, you could say that The Prestige is its own kind of magic trick. The reason why viewers feel that way is because director Christopher Nolan invites us to examine his movie from that perspective in its opening moments.

Michael Caine plays Cutter, an expert in magic who starts the film by explaining how a magic trick works. We learn that a trick consists of three parts: the pledge (the magician shows you something seemingly ordinary); the turn (the magician makes the ordinary thing do something extraordinary); and the prestige (the payoff of the trick). Cutter also explains the philosophy behind why audiences love magic tricks: We'll try to figure out how the magician did it but, at the same time, we love being wowed by the illusion. As he puts it, "You want to be fooled."

In the opening minutes of The Prestige, Nolan has essentially dared us to see if we can spot the sleight-of-hand he's executing. And, indeed, there are extraordinary twists in this thriller. The movie foreshadows the surety that there will be surprises, but can we figure out how Nolan did it?

Plastic Images

Infusing inanimate objects with emotional or symbolic meaning – because, sometimes, a cigar is most certainly not just a cigar

Almost every movie uses props, which can range from weapons to artifacts to musical instruments to fantastical creations. But some props are more important to a story than others. Here, we'll examine what I'll call "plastic images," which are objects that represent a film's theme or emotional underpinning.

The most famous plastic image in all of cinema is probably in *Citizen Kane*. That entire film is devoted to understanding precisely why Charles Foster Kane whispered "Rosebud" before his death. What was "Rosebud"? Why did it matter so much to him? When we learn that Rosebud was his sled, we stop seeing it as just a childhood toy – it's suddenly infused with profound meaning.

The movies have all sorts of plastic images. Unlocking their narrative import goes a long way towards understanding a film's underlying message.

A symbol of hope

Bicycle Thieves
1948
Screenplay: Cesare
Zavattini; director:
Vittorio De Sica; actors:
Lamberto Maggiorani,
Enzo Staiola

In Vittorio De Sica's 1948 classic, Lamberto Maggiorani plays Antonio, who has landed a menial job that requires him using a bicycle. Unfortunately, Antonio's family is poor, so they sell some items to buy back his bike from a pawnshop. *Bicycle Thieves* is the story of what happens after Antonio's bicycle then gets stolen, which involves him and his adoring son (Enzo Staiola) traveling across Rome trying to apprehend the thief.

The film examines life in postwar Italy, especially for its most marginalized citizens, and it's also a study of a father and a son. That bicycle becomes a critical storytelling element. Early on, the bike represents hope for Antonio, who just wants to make some money to support his family. As a result, when he loses the bicycle, the theft is incredibly emotional – Antonio is losing a financial lifeline. Additionally, the stolen bike can be seen as an indication of his failure as a husband and father. Antonio isn't simply seeking the bicycle – he's trying to restore his sense of self-worth.

Bicycle Thieves illustrates how a plastic image can be incredibly resonant. This movie may be a simple story about a search for a bike, but we understand how much more complicated it is for this man. And near the film's finale, when he tries to steal someone else's bike, the shame and tragedy of the scene is pointed. It represents a fall from grace for Antonio, who has given into the temptation of being as crooked and immoral as others around him.

A darker meaning

Inception
2010
Screenplay: Christopher Nolan; director: Christopher Nolan; actor: Leonardo DiCaprio

Filmmakers can infuse benign, everyday objects with darker meaning because of the context of their stories. Take, for instance, *Inception*, which follows Leonardo DiCaprio's Dom Cobb and his team of thieves, who go into the subconscious of their targets to steal or insert ideas. Such a sci-fi premise requires complicated rules, and writer–director Christopher Nolan dazzles us with the intricacy of his tale.

But much of *Inception* rides on a simple, but ominous conceit: Dom knows that he's still in the world of dreams if he spins a small top and it permanently twirls. (If he's back in the real world, gravity takes hold and the top eventually stops.) That's a clever story beat, but we become invested in the top because, for Dom, reality is sometimes less appealing than the subconscious – and he may be tempted to enter the dream world permanently once he realizes that his dead wife Mal (Marion Cotillard) lives there.

The deeper we go into *Inception*, the more confused we get about which realm we're in – dreams or reality – and so the top becomes our only guide. Likewise, this plastic image represents Dom's tentative grasp on the real world. When he's awake, he must face the fact that his wife is gone and that he may never see his children again. When he's in the dream world, she's still alive and anything is possible. That's why *Inception*'s ending is so shocking: We think Dom is happy at last, but is he awake or asleep? Fully conscious or in deep denial? The spinning top leaves us wondering, anxious.

A voice for the voiceless

The Piano
1993
Screenplay: Jane
Campion; director:
Jane Campion; actors:
Holly Hunter, Anna Paquin

If a character cannot speak, how can she communicate with the world? In the case of *The Piano*, the mute Ada (Oscar-winner Holly Hunter) expresses what's within her soul through a piano, her most prized possession. And we are catching this character at an emotionally fraught moment: As the film begins, Ada is to be married to the ineffectual Alisdair (Sam Neill), but she catches the eye of his neighbor and friend Barnes (Harvey Keitel).

Writer–director Jane Campion, who was awarded Best Original Screenplay, uses Ada's piano for several narrative purposes. On a most basic level, the piano provides Ada with a way to convey deep longing and passion through her majestic playing. More profoundly, though, the piano is an extension of Ada – so much so that she's wounded when Alisdair resists bringing the piano to his small house. Along the same lines, Barnes understands that showing an interest in the piano is the same as showing interest in Ada. When Ada plays for Barnes, it's a kind of courtship, almost a mating ritual.

The piano of *The Piano* continues to be a crucial plastic image throughout the story, and what happens to it sometimes mirrors what occurs to Ada. In this film's desolate, cruel New Zealand locale, the piano is a rare example of grace and beauty, just like the woman who plays it. We become as invested in the piano's fate as we do Ada's.

Antagonists and Obstacles

Determining the external and internal forces that are trying to hold your protagonist back

Everyone loves a hero, but a character is only as mighty as the villain he's battling. No one would care about James Bond if he was just helping kittens out of trees: To prove your mettle, you have to square off against the most fiendish, the most diabolical, the most evil of nemeses. When crafting a compelling protagonist, you need to think about the ideal archenemy for your hero as well. But your protagonist's greatest challenge isn't just an external foe. Sometimes, his toughest opponent is within.

When we talk about antagonists and obstacles, we refer to two separate hostile forces. But both are important.

An enemy who looks you in the eye

The Empire Strikes Back
1980
Screenplay: Lawrence Kasdan and Leigh Brackett; director: Irvin Kershner; actors: Mark Hamill, David Prowse

A film's antagonist is usually pretty easy to spot: He's the bad guy. A classic example of an antagonist is Darth Vader (voiced by James Earl Jones), who is trying to crush the Rebellion, led by Luke Skywalker (Mark Hamill). The original *Star Wars* trilogy is very much a showdown between protagonist and antagonist, between good and evil. There are twists along the way – Luke discovers Darth Vader's true identity – but George Lucas's space adventure gives us a clear villain who tries to keep our hero from achieving his goals. In 1980's *The Empire Strikes Back*, these opposing forces literally clash in the film's climactic lightsaber battle. The antagonist is an external individual who must be defeated.

The internal obstacles that hold you back

Rocky
1976
Screenplay: Sylvester Stallone; director: John G. Avildsen; actor: Sylvester Stallone

Sometimes the opposing force isn't just an individual; it's something within the main character that he must vanquish. In the classic sports drama and underdog tale *Rocky*, Rocky Balboa is a regular guy with a big heart who always wondered what might have happened if he'd applied himself as a boxer. The obvious nemesis in the film is Apollo Creed (Carl Weathers), the strutting boxing champ who gives lowly Rocky a title bout as a way to stir up publicity. But *Rocky* also features another, perhaps even more imposing, obstacle, which isn't so easily visible.

As we'll discover over the course of the film, the so-called Italian Stallion once had promise as a boxer, but never lived up to his potential. Now that this opportunity to fight Apollo has fallen into his lap, he has to do more than get into peak physical shape; he has to sharpen up mentally. His trainer Mickey (Burgess Meredith) has to help Rocky conquer an internal obstacle – his fear that he's not good enough, that he's wasted his life, that he'll always just be a bum. When Rocky takes on Apollo, he's not simply battling the world champ: He's fighting his own demons.

Rocky finds a clever way to dramatize that inner struggle. One of the film's most indelible moments occurs when Rocky is running through the streets of Philadelphia, eventually sprinting up the steps of the Museum of Art and holding his arms out in triumph. He hasn't even faced Apollo yet but, in a sense, he's already a winner. The moment externalizes the battle he's been waging within himself, and his exultant expression indicates that he's no longer held down by those old fears.

Invisible addictions stronger than any external foe

Requiem for a Dream
2000
Screenplay: Darren
Aronofsky and Hubert
Selby Jr.; director: Darren
Aronofsky; actors: Jared
Leto, Jennifer Connelly

Not all movies have a clearly defined bad guy. Just as in real life, some movie characters are simply battling themselves – and they're losing the fight.

Consider *Requiem for a Dream*, which is based on Hubert Selby Jr.'s 1970s novel about drug addiction. The film focuses on several characters, including lovers Harry (Jared Leto) and Marion (Jennifer Connelly), who are hooked on heroin. The movie doesn't feature a Darth Vader or an Apollo Creed – the obstacles are entirely the characters' inability to get clean. (In fact, they're often consumed with getting *more* drugs.)

On a narrative level, such internal obstacles can be challenging to dramatize. At least movies such as *Star Wars* and *Rocky* give the viewer clear rooting interests and cut-and-dried conflicts. But director Darren Aronofsky chooses to explore addiction's hold on these characters, plunging the audience into an immersive, kinetic approximation of what drug dependence feels like. This startling, upsetting film is a reminder that storytellers don't need to give their characters an obvious external foe to confront. Our hero's greatest nemesis may be staring back at him in the mirror.

Theme

Expressing the ideas occurring inside the plot

A story draws us in for many reasons. Maybe the plot sounds interesting. Perhaps it's a genre we enjoy. But, often, what makes us return to a film again and again is what's happening underneath the plot. We become fascinated not in what happens in that film but, rather, what the film's about.

A simple shorthand for this is a movie's theme, which is a collection of ideas and attitudes that the filmmakers are trying to impart about the subject matter. Screenwriter Craig Mazin once put it this way: "Theme is your central dramatic argument. ... I think sometimes people misunderstand the use of theme in this context and they think a theme for a screenplay could be brotherhood. Well, no. Because there's nothing to argue about there. There's no way to answer that question one way or the other. It's just a vague concept. ... Screenplays without arguments feel empty and pointless. You will probably get some version of the following note. 'What is this about? I mean, I know what it's about, but what is it *about*? Why should this movie exist? What is the point of all this?'"

In other words, it's not enough to have a smartly scripted story – knowing what it is you want to say is also important.

The idea at the center of a blockbuster

The Avengers
2012
Screenplay: Joss Whedon;
director: Joss Whedon;
actors: Scarlett
Johansson, Chris
Hemsworth, Chris Evans,
Jeremy Renner, Robert
Downey Jr., Mark Ruffalo

Even big event movies can have themes. Plenty of action films are, at their core, advocating the need for good to triumph over evil. It's a theme that resonates with audiences beyond the general excitement of spectacle and explosions. For instance, *The Avengers* (written and directed by Joss Whedon) preaches the importance of teamwork in order to accomplish difficult goals. In this 2012 blockbuster, a group of superheroes who are used to working on their own must band together to defeat the evil Loki (Tom Hiddleston). As mighty as they are individually, they're more powerful as a unit.

Obviously, lots of people would go to a superhero movie just because of the iconic characters. But by imbuing *The Avengers* with deeper ideas – namely, that even superheroes need to rely on one another to achieve a difficult goal – there's an emotional undercurrent to the film that gives it resonance.

One movie,
multiple themes

The Social Network
2010
Screenplay: Aaron Sorkin;
director: David Fincher;
actors: Jesse Eisenberg,
Justin Timberlake

A film like *The Social Network* has so many themes that different viewers can respond to different ones. Based on the founding of Facebook, this 2010 film stars Jesse Eisenberg as Mark Zuckerberg, a bright but prickly Harvard student who will create the social media giant in his dorm room. Directed by David Fincher and scripted by Aaron Sorkin, *The Social Network* concerns Mark's attempts to get his business off the ground, along the way squaring off with competitors, battling lawsuits and alienating a close friend in the form of his loyal classmate Eduardo Saverin (Andrew Garfield). But those are all merely plot points – none of that details what the film is actually *about*. That's where theme comes in.

It's a strength of *The Social Network* that several ideas power the narrative. One is the allure of popularity. As the film begins, Mark is portrayed as arrogant and aloof – and not particularly well-liked (his girlfriend dumps him in the opening sequence because he treats her so poorly). Not invited to any of Harvard's elite secret societies, he creates Facebook in part to boost his self-esteem, and to prove to others that he's somebody. From there, much of what happens in *The Social Network* is driven by his desire to be admired – or, more accurately, to be "cool," a reason why he's so easily sucked into the orbit of the smooth-talking but ethically slippery entrepreneur Sean Parker (Justin Timberlake). As much as he tries, Mark will never be popular in the way he wants; the insecurities he feels can't be wiped away, even when Facebook makes him a billionaire.

A movie's underlying themes may or may not be noticed by a viewer. What's important is that a theme gives a story its emotional or intellectual oomph.

Finding themes along the way

Free Solo
2018
Directors: Elizabeth Chai
Vasarhelyi and Jimmy Chin

While it's important to think about your story's underlying themes at the start of the writing process, sometimes those deeper ideas emerge during the filmmaking process. As an example, let's look at 2018's Oscar-winning documentary, *Free Solo*.

What's generally interesting about nonfiction filmmaking is that, while directors have ideas of what they want to focus on, surprises can arise while following the subject, which force the movie to go in new directions. *Free Solo* is about Alex Honnold, a world-class free-solo climber (meaning he scales mountains without the assistance of ropes or other apparatuses). It's a perilous activity, and watching him in *Free Solo* is nerve-racking and exhilarating.

But filmmakers Elizabeth Chai Vasarhelyi and Jimmy Chin had to make room for new themes once the cameras started rolling. For one thing, the driven, solitary Honnold began dating Sanni McCandless, and their relationship got serious while *Free Solo* was being made. And so, the documentary evolved to explore how Honnold balances his aspirations and his personal life – a struggle that many viewers can appreciate, even if we're never planning on climbing a mountain.

This theme gives *Free Solo* an emotional wallop as Honnold prepares to scale the dangerous El Capitan formation. He's not just risking his life but also threatening his loving relationship with McCandless, leaving audiences to debate his ambitions. Is he being selfish by climbing El Cap? Or should McCandless be supportive and understand that he's chasing his dream? Most viewers will see *Free Solo* because of Honnold's dangerous passion – but this unexpected theme will give them a lot to chew on during the movie.

Further Reading

Justin Chang, *FilmCraft: Editing* (Ilex Press, 2012)

Roger Ebert, *Roger Ebert's Book of Film: From Tolstoy to Tarantino, the Finest Writing From a Century of Film* (W.W. Norton, 1996)

Mike Goodridge, *FilmCraft: Directing* (Ilex Press, 2012)

Mike Goodridge and Tim Grierson, *FilmCraft: Cinematography* (Ilex Press, 2011)

Tim Grierson, *FilmCraft: Screenwriting* (Ilex Press, 2013)

Fionnuala Halligan, *FilmCraft: Production Design* (Ilex Press, 2012)

Ian Haydn Smith, *The Short Story of Film: A Pocket Guide to Key Genres, Films, Techniques and Movements* (Laurence King Publishing, 2020)

Spike Lee with Lisa Jones, *Do the Right Thing (A Fireside Book)* (Simon & Schuster, 1989)

Little White Lies, *The Little White Lies Guide to Making Your Own Movie in 39 Steps* (Laurence King Publishing, 2017)

Geoffrey Macnab and Sharon Swart, *FilmCraft: Producing* (Ilex Press, 2013)

David Parkinson, *100 Ideas That Changed Film* (Laurence King Publishing, 2012; mini edition 2019)

Richard Schickel, *Conversations with Scorsese* (Alfred A. Knopf, 2011)

Christine Vachon with David Edelstein, *Shooting to Kill: How an Independent Producer Blasts Through the Barriers to Make Movies That Matter* (HarperCollins, 1998)

Mitchell Zuckoff, *Robert Altman: The Oral Biography* (Alfred A. Knopf, 2009)

Index

Picture Credits

8/9 Universal/Kobal/Shutterstock 11 Columbia/Kobal/Shutterstock
12 Moviestore/Shutterstock 13 Dreamworks/20th Century Fox/Kobal/
Shutterstock 15 Moviestore/Shutterstock 16 Moviestore/Shutterstock
17 Michele K Short/Universal/Kobal/Shutterstock 19 Moviestore/
Shutterstock 20 Kobal/Shutterstock 21 Van Redin/Paramount/Detour
Filmproduction/Kobal/Shutterstock 23 Warner Bros/Kobal/Shutterstock
24 Moviestore/Shutterstock 25 Universal/Kobal/Shutterstock
27 Moviestore/Shutterstock 28 Focus/Kobal/Shutterstock 29 Lee Daniels/
Kobal/Shutterstock 31 Scott Green/HBO/Fine Line Features/Kobal/
Shutterstock 32 BBC Films/Kobal/Shutterstock 33 Institute Of Intellectual
Development/Kobal/Shutterstock 34/35 Photo by Michael Ochs Archives/
Getty Images 37 Universal/Kobal/Shutterstock 38 Recorded Picture
Company/Kobal/Shutterstock 39 Curiosa Films/Kobal/Shutterstock
41 David Bornfriend/Kobal/Shutterstock 42 Warner Bros/First National/
Kobal/Shutterstock 43 Zoetrope/United Artists/Kobal/Shutterstock
45 Greg Williams/Focus Features/Kobal/Shutterstock 46 Moviestore/
Shutterstock 47 TT Film/Vega Film/Zero Friction Film/Kobal/Shutterstock
49 Snap/Shutterstock 50 Moviestore/Shutterstock 51 Annapurna Pictures/
Kobal/Shutterstock 53 United Artists/Kobal/Shutterstock 54 Specta/Kobal/
Shutterstock 55 Columbia/Kobal/Shutterstock 57 Moviestore/Shutterstock
58 Kobal/Shutterstock 59 Paramount/Kobal/Shutterstock 61 Alan
Markfield/New Line Prods/Kobal/Shutterstock 62 Moviestore/Shutterstock
63 RKO/Kobal/Shutterstock 65 Studio Canal/Shutterstock 66 Peter
Mountain/Dreamworks/Warner Bros/Kobal/Shutterstock 67 Jet Tone
Prodns/Kobal/Shutterstock 68 Laurie Sparham/Miramax/Universal/Kobal/
Shutterstock 69 Selznick/MGM/Kobal/Shutterstock 70 Warner Bros/Kobal/
Shutterstock 71 Moviestore/Shutterstock 73 Canalplus/Kobal/Shutterstock
74 Relativity Media/Kobal/Shutterstock 75 See-Saw/Kobal/Shutterstock
77 Paramount/Kobal/Shutterstock 78 UGC/Studio Canal+/Kobal/
Shutterstock 79 Marvel Enterprises/20th Century Fox/Kobal/Shutterstock
81 Cino Del Duca/Pce/Lyre/Kobal/Shutterstock 82 Participant Media/
Shutterstock 83 Bruce Birmelin/Ghoulardi/New Line/Revolution/Kobal/
Shutterstock 84/85 MGM/Kobal/Shutterstock 87 Alex Kahle/RKO/Kobal/
Shutterstock 88 20th Century Fox/Kobal/Shutterstock 89 Nouvelle Edition
Francaise/Kobal/Shutterstock 91 Paramount/Kobal/Shutterstock
92 Universal/Kobal/Shutterstock 93 Snap/Shutterstock 95 Steve Dietl/
Netflix/Kobal/Shutterstock 96 American Playhouse/WMG/Geechee/Kobal/
Shutterstock 97 BBC Films/Kobal/Shutterstock 99 Kimberley French/
Warner Bros/Plan B/Scott Free/Kobal/Shutterstock 100 Lucasfilm/
Walt Disney Studios/Moviestore/Shutterstock 101 Jonathan Olley/Snap
Stills/Shutterstock 103 Redbud/Kobal/Shutterstock 104 Snap Stills/
Shutterstock 105 Moviestore/Shutterstock 107 Moviestore/Shutterstock
108 Warner Bros/Seven Arts/Tatira-Hiller Productions/Kobal/Shutterstock

109 Warner Bros/Village Roadshow Pictures/Kobal/Shutterstock
111 With thanks and acknowledgment to Columbia Pictures (screengrab)
112 With thanks and acknowledgment to the Irish Film Board (screengrab)
113 With thanks and acknowledgement to Paramount Pictures/Blumhouse Productions/Solana Films (screengrab) **115** Warner Bros/Hawk Films/Kobal/Shutterstock **116** Cottonwood/Kobal/Shutterstock **117** Fox Searchlight/New Regency/Le Grisbi/Kobal/Shutterstock **119** Brian Hamill/Tri-Star/Kobal/Shutterstock **120** Christine Plenus/Canal+/La Wallonie/Casa Kafka/Kobal/Shutterstock **121** Artisan Pics/Kobal/Shutterstock **123** Snap Stills/Shutterstock **124** Moviestore/Shutterstock **125** Bazelevs Prods/Versus/Kobal/Shutterstock **127** With thanks and acknowledgment to Warner Bros/Wildwood Enterprises (screengrab) **128** With thanks and acknowledgment to Paramount Pictures (screengrab) **129** With thanks and acknowledgment to The Weinstein Company (screengrab) **131** Big Talk Productions/Kobal/Shutterstock **132** Merrick Morton/20th Century Fox/Regency/Kobal/Shutterstock **133** Elliott Marks/Red Mullet Prod/Kobal/Shutterstock
135 With thanks and acknowledgment to Warner Bros (screengrab)
136 With thanks and acknowledgment to Lucasfilm/Bad Robot/Walt Disney Studios (screengrab) **137** With thanks and acknowledgment to Hollywood/Wildwood/Baltimore (screengrab) **138/139** Photo by Steve Schapiro/Corbis via Getty Images **141** With thanks and acknowledgment to Focus Features (screengrab) **142** With thanks and acknowledgment to Lucasfilm/20th Century Fox (screengrab) **143** With thanks and acknowledgment to Universal/Gordon (screengrab) **145** With thanks and acknowledgment to Columbia (screengrab) **146** With thanks and acknowledgment to MGM/Stanley Kubrick Productions (screengrab) **147** With thanks and acknowledgment to MGM (screengrab) **149** Lucasfilm/Fox/Kobal/Shutterstock **150** Warner Bros/Kobal/Shutterstock **151** Warner Bros/Kobal/Shutterstock **153** With thanks and acknowledgment to UGC (screengrab) **154** With thanks and acknowledgment to Touchstone Pictures (screengrab) **155** With thanks and acknowledgment to Zentropa (screengrabs) **157** Paramount/Kobal/Shutterstock **158** Eon/Danjaq/Sony/Kobal/Shutterstock **159** Clay Enos/Warner Bros/Kobal/Shutterstock **160/161** Bettmann/Getty **163** Castle Rock/Nelson/Columbia/Kobal/Shutterstock **164** James Bridges/Sweetland/Kobal/Shutterstock **165** Moviestore/Shutterstock **167** Moviestore/Shutterstock **168** Warner Bros/Kobal/Shutterstock **169** Groundswell Prods/Kobal/Shutterstock **171** Paramount/Kobal/Shutterstock **172** Warner Bros/Kobal/Shutterstock **173** Moviestore/Shutterstock **175** Produzione De Sica/Kobal/Shutterstock **176** Warner Bros/Kobal/Shutterstock **177** Jan Chapman Prods/Miramax/Kobal/Shutterstock **179** Lucasfilm/Fox/Kobal/Shutterstock **180** Moviestore/Shutterstock **181** Moviestore/Shutterstock **183** Marvel Enterprises/Kobal/Shutterstock **184** Columbia/Kobal/Shutterstock **185** J Chin/National Geographic/Kobal/Shutterstock

Acknowledgments

I'd like to thank Zara Larcombe for suggesting such a terrific idea in the first place, and Felicity Maunder for guiding the book so capably.

This Is How You Make a Movie would not have been written without the endless support of my wife Susan Stoebner, whose enthusiasm for film and keen insights have helped shape my own thoughts for nearly two decades. Filmmaker and friend John Baumgartner gave the book a careful proofread, challenging some of my assumptions and offering plenty of encouragement. Both were very much appreciated.

But this book is dedicated to my parents, Debbie and Bob, who let me go to film school so long ago. In some ways, I wrote *This Is How You Make a Movie* for my younger self, who would have loved such a helpful guide to film's complex architecture. Thanks for believing, Mom and Dad.